CHRIS HANNAN

Chris Hannan was born in Glasgow. His other plays include *The Orphans' Comedy* (1986), *Elizabeth Gordon Quinn* (1985) and *Klimkov: Life of a Tsarist Agent* (1984), all of which were first produced at the Traverse Theatre, Edinburgh. Currently, he is writing a new play for the National Theatre as well as working on a translation of Ibsen's *The Pretenders* for the RSC. He was voted Most Promising Playwright in the 1990 Plays and Players' Critics' Poll and nominated for a Charrington's London Fringe Award.

by the same author

Elizabeth Gordon Quinn
(in *Scot-Free* edited by Alasdair Cameron)

THE EVIL DOERS
&
THE BABY

Two Plays by
CHRIS HANNAN

NICK HERN BOOKS

A Nick Hern Book

The Evil Doers first published in 1991 as an original paperback by Nick Hern Books, a Random Century Company, 20 Vauxhall Bridge Road, London SW1V 2SA

Front cover illustration: *x-chen* 1938 (x-let) brush drawing by Paul Klee. Reproduced by kind permission of Angela Rosengart, Lucerne.

Set in Baskerville by 🅐 Tek Art Ltd,
Addiscombe, Croydon, Surrey
Printed by T J Press

British Library Cataloguing in Publication Data
Hannan, Chris
   The evil doers and the baby
   1. English drama
   I. Title
   822.914

ISBN: 85459–100–2

Contents

Introduction

I'm quite happy if these two plays seem very different. I'd be delighted if people thought they were by two different people. To me, the same rules apply in theatre as apply in company, and to avoid repeating yourself is just basic courtesy. You repeat yourself anyway, because you can't help it, but the whole point of being in company is to get outside yourself, to party.

In the theatre that means telling a good story, in whatever way.

The embryonic idea for *The Baby* was that a group of professional mourners would be asked to mourn the death of someone they hated. I didn't know where I would set the story. At first I thought India or the Caribbean, but then I started to read up some Roman history and came across Sulla.

As a political leader Sulla was much loved and much hated. He was loved because he succeeded in cutting inflation and interest rates and restoring public order. He was hated because he achieved this by cutting public expenditure, principally the doles. So when he died there was controversy about whether or not he should get a state funeral.

This seemed a good enough start, and when I put my imaginary professional mourners in the middle of this emotionally and politically divided city and then threw in a deeply disturbed Pompey and a (historically) gratuitous riot, I had a context and situation which appealed to me. I wanted to create mess; chaos; a situation where emotions outrun or shortcircuit or otherwise cut across the objective political forces at work.

The intention, then, is anti-Brechtian but not apolitical; it's anti-Brechtian because I think Brecht is politically shallow.

The Baby is the story of Macu on the one hand and Pompey on the other, both of whom bring to the political conflict their own ghostly and unexplored griefs. The story starts with them and ends with them, as individuals, because that's what I was interested in; Macu's anger; Pompey's emotional disconnection. As it happens, I identified with both of them, though I accept that audiences will side with Macu. Maybe to restore the balance, I gave Pompey both Marcella *and* Sorcha so that at least *on*-stage he will have people who love him.

I focused on the characters because I thought it would give the

audience a richer experience politically too. I don't want them to
abstract the political dimension, I want them to experience it.

The process of writing these two plays couldn't have been more
different. *The Baby* was long and difficult and a bit of a monster,
and it's only now, having just completed its fourth major re-draft,
that I feel reasonably satisfied with it. Whereas *The Evil Doers* was
comparatively painless.

I wanted to write something in a contemporary setting and
Glasgow 1990 was coming up, which I thought it would be good
to exploit. I liked the idea of a City Comedy which would move
around the place and came up with the idea of Sammy and his
city-wide Taxi Tours. Then I had the idea of a daughter who
hated him and wanted to sabotage his business. And finally I
came up with the thing which explained both these characters
and also their antagonism: the alcoholic who dominates their
thoughts.

I felt lucky. In a Glasgow river-side club called 'Panama Jax', a
pleasant and bright-faced young man at another table started
talking to me. At a certain point in the conversation, I asked him
what he did. He said he was a Nazi, he just followed orders. I
asked him what he meant. He said he was a criminal. I asked him
what area of criminality he specialised in. He was a loanshark.
The conversation ran aground at that point, but I was glad to
have met him. I already had a loanshark in my story by this time,
but the self-consciousness of the bright-faced young man
influenced the writing of Tex. Characters are one thing, but
more importantly I also seemed to luck on a story-structure
which was simple and also had a dynamic that expressed the
family dynamic.

It still took me nine months to write a first draft though, nine-
tenths of which I subsequently ditched . . . But once the team at
The Bush had lanced the suppurating boil I called the sub-plot (a
member of a right-wing Think-Tank with a plan to bring the
Foreign Office and half the government to Glasgow on the sound
economic grounds of easing inflationary congestion in the South
East), the second draft was plain (ish) sailing. The dynamic of the
story-line emerged more strongly and I began to enjoy *in detail*
the running dog-fight round Glasgow that's the core of the play.

I should say that I had no intention of writing a play about
Glasgow, or about the City of Culture; that was the excuse for the
play not its subject. The whole Taxi Tour element is a structural
diversion, just as Glasgow is a substitute object of love, Sammy's
belle dame sans merci, a woman he finds himself making love to
because Agnes is even more inaccessible. So when Agnes, drunk,

face cut, tights ripped, says 'I'm Glasgow', this is Agnes talking, not the playwright. She's trying to get at Sammy, and because she's an alcoholic she homes in like a smart bomb on the weakest point of his structure.

In both plays I was writing for the open stage. As much as possible, the characters bring the location on with them, they bring the scene. I like the movement this allows and the visual interest, and it puts the responsibility on me to make sure that what comes on to the stage is active. In design terms this implies that what comes on to the stage should have more emphasis than the set, or at least should read strongly against the set. From the writing point of view, it means that not only should the characters be active, but the props should be active too, and more expressive than they might need to be in another kind of play. Sometimes the props don't do much more than denote an action, as in *The Baby* when Macu and Emilia come on pushing loot in a pram. But when Emilia then produces a doll to give to Laura, this is something else, more alive, as the wreaths are in the opening riot scene or the stretcher is in the last scene of the first act. Anyway, I'm telling you this simply because it was a part of the writing I enjoyed. I like to get people and props on and off stage without recourse to blackouts.

Usually when I write something, in my head I'm writing it *for* someone, usually more than one person, but maybe for one person in particular.

The one person in particular that *The Evil Doers* is for, is Cathie Hannan.

The one person in particular that *The Baby* is for, is Louise Donald.

Chris Hannan

Edinburgh, 1991.

THE EVIL DOERS

Every single time I want to do good, something evil comes to hand.

(Rom. 7:21)

The Evil Doers was first staged at the Bush Theatre, London on 31 August 1990, with the following cast:

TRACKY	Sharon Muircroft
SUSAN	Katy Murphy
SAMMY	Tom Mannion
TEX	Douglas Henshall
TOURIST	Lucy Aston
LUCY	Lucy Aston
AGNES	Alison Peebles

Directed by Simon Usher
Designed by Anthony Lamble
Lighting by Ace McCarron

A new production of *The Evil Doers* by the Winged Horse Theatre Company directed by Hamish Glen opened at the Byre Theatre, St Andrews on 2 May 1991 and transferred to the Mitchell Theatre Glasgow on 7 May 1991.

ACT ONE

Scene One

*Bridge over the Expressway. A glass thing with red steel ribcage.
SUSAN and TRACKY saunter on. Both are about fifteen. Both are
heavy metal fans, and wear the leather jackets etc.*

TRACKY. So what did they say?

SUSAN. I told you.

TRACKY. Did they say you weren't to go back?

That's what I'd've said. I'd've said away back to the swamp,
swamp brain.

I thought you didn't want a baby.

SUSAN. I don't.

TRACKY. So – right.

SUSAN. I'm only fifteen. I've got my whole career ahead of me.

TRACKY. Well then!

SUSAN. Well then! – that's three times in the last five months
I've been negative. Why is everything so dead negative. I try
being like positive. Like we're all going to die anyway so what's
it matter, right? – but that only cheers me up for about three
seconds. Know what I thought last night? I was lying in my pit
and I'm thinking about the universe, because that's much more
important than we are, right? And I thought: I'm like the
discarded larva of a gigantic Zardoid ant.

Pause.

TRACKY. I wish you'd use contraceptives.

SUSAN. I know.

TRACKY. It's completely irresponsible, Susan.

SUSAN. I've got a lot on my mind right now, Tracky!

2 THE EVIL DOERS

TRACKY. Like what?

SUSAN. Like! – Oh god, Tracky, what if I'm infertile? Oh god, I'm so *tragic!* D'you think I should get a test? Quick, come we'll go: I feel faint.

TRACKY. Go where?

SUSAN. Quick – I don't know what we're doing here, we're inside someone's ribcage.

TRACKY. Are you about to throw a flakey, ya creep?

SUSAN. Look – there's your Da.

TRACKY (*upset*). Because don't make things up, Susan.

SUSAN. Down there, there's his taxi.

TRACKY. *Not as fast as that!*

SUSAN. Calm down, we're all going to die anyway, what's it matter?

TRACKY. I don't like lies.

SUSAN. You should change your prescription, Tracky.

TRACKY. We're on a bridge over the Expressway going to the Exhibition Centre. It's just got red steel metal –

She draws rib-shaped metal things in the air.

ribs.

SUSAN. Come we'll go annoy him.

TRACKY. Who?

SUSAN. Your Da! Don't be so pedestrian – he's down there trying to chat up some tourists.

Still suspicious, TRACKY *goes to look.*

There.

TRACKY *sees him.*

TRACKY. So what. That's his job.

SUSAN. That is so *weird.*

Beat.

TRACKY. He just looks like *somebody.*

SUSAN. Let's go see him: this is meant to be, Tracky. We're just kicking about like lost in space the night after a rock concert and then we see your Da!? – I'm going.

And she goes. TRACKY *looks down at the somebody that's her Da, as the scene changes round about her. Then she follows* SUSAN.

Scene Two

Outside. Hot day. Finnieston Quayside. A young man comes on, twenty-one at most, in a good suit. He's carrying a red toolbox. This is TEX. *He stands watching someone offstage. Then he sees the someone approaching. He smiles, puts the toolbox down and waits.*
On comes SAMUEL DOAK *in jeans and T-shirt. He's carrying a hoarding, which says 'Danny Glasgow's Taxi Tours' in Rennie Mackintosh lettering, and a cellnet phone. He's thirty-seven. He's the husband of an alcoholic – and this shows itself in his physical tension and mental distraction.*

SAMMY. Don't waste *her* time? Don't waste *her* time? (Hotel receptionist) calm as you like she said it – I've been standing looking at (clock right behind her!) for thirty-five minutes! It's one of those clocks looks like it's got all the time in the world. Cool green marble thing. And the hotel receptionist, she's cool. She's got the grey skirt and the smart white blouse on, hasn't she. She's got the all-over-air-conditioned body.

Still. This is me now. Danny Glasgow. The wide open spaces. – Are you – ?

Just been in at the hotel there, picking up a few fares. Ahch, they never showed. – Fucking tourists. Because I *love* this city. I *love* this city. I actually *love* it. That's what you can't communicate to them . . . Glasgow.

Ah well. Happy happy happy, so long as *I'm* happy. – So, no offence. I'll make my pitch here – this is the way the tourists come. No offence.

TEX. Let me ask you a question. Do you know me?

Pause.

SAMMY. How? *Do* I know you?

TEX. You tell me. Do you *know* me?

SAMMY. Not to my knowledge. Not unless you're (who I think you are). Are you?

TEX. Because from the way you were prattling on like a pranny, I was surmising you knew me.

SAMMY. I talk to any bastard! That's why they call it the Friendly City, isn't it: talk to any bastard.

TEX. So I'm a stranger to you.

SAMMY. Far as I know.

TEX. Then how come I know you?

SAMMY. Haw.

TEX. Ih?

SAMMY. Come on. Danny Glasgow: I'm advertised.

TEX. Samuel, Samuel: I'm not talking rubbish here. That's the *first* time I've called your name today. The third time I call your name, you're dead. Because you're not listening; you're not listening to yourself, you're estranged from your conscience. Then I come along and you don't know who I am.

TEX picks up his toolbox.

TEX. Suit: what am I doing with a toolbox? – Today's the day, my friend. Money.

TEX exits.

SAMMY. This is my lucky pitch.

He says this in the direction in which TEX has gone.

Underneath the big crane here. I come here, bit of bother, say a wee prayer to the big crane and bingo: tourists.

Sound of SUSAN screaming off. SAMMY has a heart attack.

Aaaaagh!

Then he sees SUSAN and TRACKY off.

The day started out perfectly hopeful too. Now I'm being attacked from the air by –

SUSAN and TRACKY arrive.

SUSAN. Hiya, Mr Doak. It's us.

SAMMY. – lamb-eating female eagles.

SUSAN. We saw you from way up there. You just looked like somebody.

SAMMY. I'm at my work here, girls.

SUSAN. I know. So wahl, so how're you getting on?

SAMMY. Fine. Fine. Stretching my legs.

SUSAN. What for?

SAMMY. Warming up. – How's Tracky?

TRACKY *is so tense she can hardly think.*

Sleep OK last night?

TRACKY (*tight-mouthed*). Yes.

SAMMY. Good – well played, well played. – So you never heard any noise then?

TRACKY. No.

SAMMY. Good. I'll phone the glaziers soon as I (get a break). Because you know your mother: a few drinks in her and she's lethal with that hammer. – So you slept then?

TRACKY (*can hardly speak*). I told you. No.

SAMMY. Good, good, so long as you slept. – And look at: are you kidding me on: on a lovely red hot roasting day like this? Look at the jackets.

SUSAN. How, what's wrong with them?

SAMMY. Wrong with them?

SUSAN. This is genuine leather, Mr Doak.

SAMMY. That pavement could fry brains. And you, Tracky: lovely well-developed girl like you? Show yourself off a bit more. We're all in Europe now.

SUSAN. Quick, Mr Doak – here's a tourist.

SAMMY. Right you pair –

SUSAN. What're you going to say to her?

SAMMY. Listen: Glasgow.

SUSAN. You can't just say that.

SAMMY. I could tell you a fact about every square metre of this city. Now scram.

SUSAN. We want to watch you, don't we, Tracky?

SAMMY. Well you can't. The tourists will take one look.

TRACKY. She's seen us. She's stopped.

SUSAN. She's got a map out.

SAMMY. I offer these people a tour round some of the city's most interesting, so will you – : and stop trying to look like muggers! (you'll spoil their concentration).

TRACKY. She's coming.

SUSAN. Can I show her the tattoo on my chest? It's a sea-serpent rising from the deep, you should see the detail that's in it.

SAMMY. Susan, will you. The tourists don't. I hope you've no detail on *your* chest, Tracky!

An American tourist comes on.

NAN. Would you excuse me?

SAMMY. Hello hello hello –

SUSAN. Hiya!

SAMMY. – welcome to the Friendly City.

SUSAN (*over* SAMMY's *shoulder*). Congratulations.

SAMMY. Don't mind her, this is my pet harpy. Haw. Look at you: map. Because away to hell, map? – this is Danny Glasgow here.

NAN. I was wondering, could you possibly tell me –

SAMMY. You want to eat, I'll show you the eateries. Browse in the past, we have the heritage facilities on-site to simulate that.

SUSAN. He's in the official brochure.

TRACKY. He paid for a whole page.

SAMMY. What's that peeking out your handbag, madam?

It's a shoulderbag and it's zipped up.

The ubiquitous plastic mac or macintosh, so called after its inventor, the Glasgow chemist Charles Macintosh . . . not to be confused with Charles *Rennie* Mackintosh, who invented the indigestion tablet (haw, I tell them *all* that joke), he actually invented art nouveau. You name it, we invented it.

NAN. I have an enquiry.

SAMMY. Kerosene? Antiseptic? Television?

NAN. I got one in my hotel-room.

SAMMY. Clichés now, history then. (Did she say hotel-room?)

NAN. (Did you say television?)

SAMMY. (Am I using too many big words for you?)

NAN. Do you have a store here called Marks and Spencer? My
   girlfriend back home, she was over here last year, she
   recommended me I should go there.

   Pause.

SAMMY. Marks and Spencer's?

NAN. I believe it's a chain-store. My girlfriend tells me it has
   excellent quality – and good prices.

SAMMY. Is it (my life!) Marks and Spencer's you're looking for?

TRACKY. The lady's asking you where's there a Marks and
   Spencer's.

SAMMY. I know what she's asking me! She's asking me have we
   got a Marks and Spencer's. Because they've got a Marks and
   Sparks in *Belfast!*

NAN. Because I got a clothes problem. I hate clothes. I see a
   garment I like, I buy a whole bunch of them, I buy the line. I
   guess I have a lazy brain.

SAMMY. Can you move along please?

NAN. Pardon me?

SAMMY. (Time's not my own.)

NAN. Well I was only making an enquiry.

SAMMY. What was it again? Do we have a Marks and Spencer's?
   Go and ask someone!

TRACKY. – shout: that's your answer to everything.

SAMMY. I get a question like that and my brain shuts down.
   Because the brain's smarter than we are: the brain (this is me
   I'm talking about): to prevent meltdown, that's why!

TRACKY. Just tell her.

SAMMY. I'm sorry, Tracky: I can't override my brain's self-defence mechanism. (I might blow up!) – All I ask for is. I know more facts than. And then you ask me where there's a Marks and Spencer's.

NAN. I guess it's the only store I heard of.

SAMMY. I appreciate that. But you see *my* problem. I'm expected to comprehend you!

NAN. Should I go? I've disturbed your equilibrium. It's OK, I do that to my husband too. I have this low brain activity which pisses him off. He says I emit brain signals that are like so weak he's not equipped to receive them. He thinks I do that on purpose. Sure I do, I don't wanna let the guy know how much I hate him.

TRACKY. You get the train from there. Get off at Argyle Street. There's a Marks's facing you.

NAN. Yeah?

SUSAN. It's dead easy.

NAN. Argyle Street? I can handle that.

SUSAN. And good luck with your clothes' problem.

NAN (*polite*). You likewise.

　She goes.

　Pause.

SAMMY. So thanks, Tracky. Thank you.

TRACKY. What did I do?

SAMMY. Family? No wonder Karl Marx wanted to abolish it.

SUSAN. You could give her a hire into town, Mr Doak.

　Beat.

SAMMY. When I think how much I know about this city I could cry. Three years I spent, nights, up in the Mitchell Library on my own, getting to know this city intimately (and time going by). Intimacy? People talk about it. It means standing at the bus-stop on your own night after night. – I'll go check the hotel see if my fares have showed up yet.

SAMMY *goes.*

TRACKY. OK, Susan. Change the subject. Because it's so boring! – Danny Glasgow. His name's Sammy Doak.

SUSAN. That's his personality, Tracky.

TRACKY. He's all over the place.

SUSAN. He's explosive! – And I think it's really courageous, like, to chuck the job he had at the chicken factory and start his own business.

TRACKY. Don't start me, Susan. It's completely irresponsible! He was a supervisor and everything.

LUCY *enters. She's 26 or so. For some time now, she has had great difficulties in constructing a personality. The only thing holding her together is a terrible determination.*

LUCY. Excuse me.

TRACKY *and* SUSAN *look her up and down.*

TRACKY. Shag off.

LUCY. Could you tell me what that crane is?

SUSAN. How?

TRACKY. Because I'm dangerous, by the way: I've been to psychiatrists.

LUCY. Oh – so have I, how interesting! – I'm a journalist, freelance. I thought, while I'm here, I might try doing a piece for *Elle*, or something. 'Of the river that once built half the world's ships, nothing now remains as a reminder of past glories' – yuck – 'except a soviet of cranes idly discussing the skyline.' I *love* writing shit. It's a fine art. – So, what do you think of Glasgow then?

Pause.

TRACKY. Donno.

SUSAN. Is this an interview?

LUCY. If it develops.

TRACKY. We don't give interviews: that's shite.

SUSAN. This is Tracky. She is bad craziness, she shagged the whole of Panic Attack. That's a band.

TRACKY. They only play pubs, because it's more real.

SUSAN. Tracky wants to put a boy off she gags down his throat.

TRACKY. Don't listen to her, she lives in a swamp.

SUSAN. I sleep with a sweaty piece of slime who can't keep his hands off me, called Chick. (I know: I'm utterly crazy.)

TRACKY. Comic-head.

SUSAN. So if I start to hyper-ventilate it's because of my provenance.

LUCY. Wonderful – 'provenance'! Your language.

SUSAN. How? Where is it *you're* from?

LUCY. Me? Oh it's boring, you wouldn't want to hear. Andover – it's where Army HQ is. Everyone's father was an admiral or brigadier or something. Terrible place – I crossed the Andes just to get away from it.

TRACKY. What paper will it be in? Because we're utterly mental, by the way, we only told you about half of it.

SAMMY *returns*.

SAMMY. I should charge them a cancellation fee. I'm too reasonable, that's my problem: I hurt myself.

SUSAN. Look, Mr Doak: here's another enquiry.

SAMMY. The nearest Woolworth's is Dumbarton Road. Now get, you two: my brain's gone dark. I blame your mother for this. That glazier knew our address without me telling him . . . (I try to use a different one each time too).

TRACKY (*embarrassed, quiet*). Can you not keep anything to yourself? (She's a journalist.)

SAMMY. He recognised my *voice!* Keep your mother to myself (I wish I could) because see your mother, Tracky, your mother's a by-word in glazier's circles. (She's a what?)

SUSAN. She's a journalist, Mr Doak.

Awful pause.

SAMMY. What have I said so far?

I apologise for Woolworth's. There's an explanation for that.

TRACKY. We were just telling her about the real Glasgow. Crazy heads.

SUSAN. Slums.

TRACKY. Razor gangs.

SUSAN. She was lapping it up, Mr Doak.

SAMMY. Haw: kids. I should report them to the pest control people. – So, you've tracked me down: Danny Glasgow. What's the angle?

LUCY. Why, is there one?

SAMMY. We've all got something to hide.

LUCY. *Interesting* people. Some people have got nothing to hide at all. I think boring people should at least try and *disguise* the fact.

SAMMY. So which are you?

Beat.

LUCY. I'm a journalist. Maybe you could help me actually. I'm trying to work up a piece about EMI. Because the word is (or so my contacts in the music biz. tell me) the *word* is, that EMI is so fed up with London costs and traffic and queues and *Sorry This Escalator is Not in Use* and the whole unbearable London thing, it's about to move to (*I* didn't believe it at first) Glasgow.

Pause.

SUSAN. EMI.

SAMMY. Glasgow? – Do you hear that, ya wee heathens? I keep telling them. Glasgow I say to them.

TRACKY. EMI.

LUCY. Well – part of it, yes. I mean, it's huge, it's a major multi-national.

SAMMY. I knew you were a dark hope soon as I saw you. And you need to flesh out the story, correct? EMI, you tack that onto the resurrection of the city as a whole, plus the lovely green low-cost environment, and (story?): tell that to the pygmies.

SUSAN. Where will they build it? Because that's not a problem.

SAMMY. Exactly.

SUSAN. Because that's one thing, we've got hunners of waste ground.

SAMMY. It's tragic really. 'Waste ground': she's living in the past. We don't have any waste ground.

SUSAN. We do so have waste ground.

SAMMY. We don't have any waste ground.

SUSAN. We do so have waste ground.

SAMMY. We do not have waste ground. We've got open space areas. Which is exactly what developers want. – Have you seen my taxi! Just newly washed her. Look at the body on her: like a seal. – So OK. Though in saying that, it'll be sore on *me*. What, just the one skull on board?

LUCY. You mean: – No I couldn't possibly. I mean: surely? You're working!

Does she think he's offering her a free trip? This causes SAMMY *to pause.*

SAMMY. To let you understand: obviously there's my running costs.

LUCY. Exactly.

SAMMY. I mean: we're talking about petrol here.

LUCY. Well yes!

SAMMY. Obscure? – she can see in the dark this one.

LUCY. Sorry?

SAMMY. Because I'm no different in that respect. Everybody's got their overheads.

LUCY. No listen: thank you for your offer, it's very kind, but I couldn't possibly cadge a free ride . . . could I? So thank you: no.

Pause, in which SAMMY *gestures incoherently, attempting to re-cast, re-write, re-negotiate the terms of this exchange.*

SAMMY. Heah. Did I mention money? Did I? Did I mention. Did you think. She thought. Because Glasgow. That's the important thing. I've got a passion for this city! I'm perfectly open about that. I'm in love with. – Eh?

LUCY. I'm not worth it, I promise you. I'm not as interesting as you think.

SAMMY. I'm thinking further ahead than (money?) I'm thinking

Scene Three

SAMMY *and* LUCY.

SAMMY. So come on come on come on (pack it in!) we've got a
lot to pack in.

LUCY. Is it always this hot?

SAMMY. This is the weather, eh? Mr Happy up there. People say
to you Spain. I know: Spain?!

LUCY. I once travelled across Spain by bus. The Spanish are
very keen on death.

SAMMY. Spain! I would say that though, wouldn't I? So if you
could just stand there, I'll show you my tourist-guide.

LUCY. Here.

SAMMY. That's lovely. And face the other way.

When LUCY *faces the other way,* SAMMY *begins his self-scripted
spiel. He reads it partly from a jotter, and partly makes it up as he goes
along.*

Ready? – So here we are in the East End of the city – and can I
just interject with the information that fifteen or so years back
this was one of the most depressed areas *in* the city. Look at it
now. 'Parkhead Forge' – this pyramid structure in glass and
steel-tubing – is the £40 million pound jewel in the East End
crown. A double-decker shopping complex with multiplex
cinema, shoppers can relax in The Courtyard Cafe with its
ecologically aware indoor trees plus the rockpink and tangerine
lighting in Yankee-style piping. And if you turn round –

She turns round, demoralised, dehumanised.

– across the road there is the Barr's Irn Bru factory, purveyors
of –

LUCY. Look, I'm sorry but –

SAMMY. Do you not see it?

LUCY. Yes. Yes. Coffee then. Shall we?

SAMMY. Because, if you could just bear with me: that's still to be
revealed yet. – The Barr's Irn Bru factory, purveyors of the
world-famous soft drink. Now – if you can picture Loch

Lomond full of Irn Bru, that's how much this factory
discharges onto the world market every single month. And on
that note, we can now adjourn to The Courtyard Cafe for our
own soft drinks . . .

He shows LUCY *the way.*

See how (trick you learn as you go along) join things up?

They go.

SUSAN *wanders on lost in space, followed by* TRACKY.

TRACKY. Where are you going, Susan; they went into the
shopping complex.

SUSAN. Did they?

TRACKY. You stood there and watched them.

SUSAN. I was thinking.

TRACKY. This is stupid. I don't even know why we came.

SUSAN. Wahl – voodoo – *that's* what I was thinking! Goldfish.
Because I read this thing, goldfish have a memory span of
about two seconds? And I thought, that is so *sad!* My wee
goldfish is swimming round his globe thinking, I wonder if . . .
I wonder if . . . I wonder if . . .

TRACKY. Creep. – It was your idea to follow them.

SUSAN. I'm not going in there. That's a shopping complex.
Shoppers are alien to me, Tracky, they all go about – shopping!
– You go. I'll stay here and watch.

TRACKY *decides to punish her.*

TRACKY. I might not come back.

SUSAN (*blank pause*). Back where?

TRACKY (*trying to 'blank pause'* SUSAN *back. Failing*). I knew
you'd say that. You're so predictable sometimes.

TRACKY *goes.*
SUSAN *sighs.*
TEX *enters.*

TEX. Susan. Susan MacAlindon. It's me – Tex.

SUSAN. Tex?

TEX. J-J. John O'Donnell.

SUSAN. Wahl. So it is. Because god.

TEX. How? Do I look different?

SUSAN. Check the outfit.

TEX. Suave?

SUSAN. Suave as fuck. I mean: blammm!

TEX. I'd to get the hair cut for the job.

SUSAN. That's what it is! You said that so dead casual too. A job!!!

TEX. So you see a difference?

SUSAN. Yeah, I'm surprised you even remember me!! I mean: remember we went to see Onslaught at the Pavilion!?

TEX. Remember? Onslaught? Heah: can I say something? Headdeath.

SUSAN. Aw man. It was some gig. Blammmm!

TEX. Nige Rockett.

TEX *lays down some heavy guitar riffs, à la Nige Rockett.*

SUSAN. Utterly crazy: 3,000 maniacs with their brains scooped out. And then they go and play 'Welcome to Dying'. It was spiritual. Fifteen minutes of pure death.

TEX. Nige Rockett.

He lays down some heavy guitar riffs à la Nige Rockett.

SUSAN. He is so *sensitive:* he's got a fear of dying. So wahl, so how are you, I'm miserable. I've just had some bad news in my personal life. Plus the fact I'm just miserable, permanent. I must take after my Mammy, she's on another planet, but I can't tell anyone, they don't have the imagination.

TEX. Aw Susan. Metal fan: you can tell me. I listen to Mordred. There's this track on their album: it's about everything.

SUSAN. It's so menial. She just lies in bed all day, zapping the telly, know how, with the remote.

And TEX *moves across to look and see if he can spot* TRACKY *or* SAMMY *coming.*

SUSAN. I told you it was menial. She doesn't even watch the programmes. She just lies in bed all day, zapping the telly, know how, with the remote. – Don't laugh, right? Yesterday I switched off the telly and hid the remote, and then I went out like all day.

Pause.

TEX. So, and what happened?

SUSAN. Nothing! Nothing happened! I know it's funny, I'm good that way, I can keep a perspective, I just wish she'd make me my tea some nights. Look what I'm reading as well. It's all about bereavement. I thought – likes of – if she tops herself – it'll be good for that, won't it? How's your lovelife, I bet it's brilliant.

TEX. Put it this way: I've no idea. I've got a kid.

SUSAN (*disappointed enthusiasm*). Awww!

TEX. Married and everything. The kid's – beautiful. Christopher.

SUSAN. Awww! That's a lovely name. So it's a boy then. And what's the job? Because you look like a manager, are you?

TEX. I work. Put it that way.

SUSAN. Is it a record shop? You're doing your manager in a record shop? Because don't tell me you work in a studio! Aw man, that's excellent.

TEX. I'm a Nazi. I just follow orders.

SUSAN. Oh god! You're not, are you!? You are – you're in a band. I don't believe it – what one, what are you called?

TEX. Susan: fuckssake man: I'm embarrassed here.

SUSAN. Tell us what you're called.

TEX. What we're called?

The Evil-Doers.

SUSAN *puts her hands over her mouth and squeals from the back of her throat.* TEX *looks around, very nervous suddenly. Decides to go.*

TEX. Listen. Here's my card. Give that to Tracky . . . likes of, if you see her. Tell her to stay out the way. I've got an appointment with her Da this morning.

And he goes. SUSAN *clutches the business card to her breast like it's a love-letter.*

TRACKY *comes back.*

TRACKY. Susan!

SUSAN. Oh Tracky: I can't tell you!

TRACKY. I think they saw me. Quick – make something up why we're here *or I'll die.*

SUSAN. Oh Tracky: I *know* why! It was meant. He's married too – oh god I am so *tragic*, I've fallen in love with a married man!

TRACKY. Remind me to copy out *your* prescription, will you?

SUSAN. It's true. He even gave me his card. He said he had business to do with your father.

She shows TRACKY *the card.*

TRACKY. Tex? That creep.

SUSAN. Read the card, Tracky, he's completely changed. He's got these really sad eyes, as if he's like trapped in a dead unhappy marriage or something. And he's in this brilliant band – the way he described it, it's like they've really come to terms with the fact that we're all going to die anyway so what's it matter –

TRACKY. He's dead.

SUSAN. Will you concentrate? – and likes of reflect that in their music. I can just see the artwork on their album. A lunar desert with all these weird cactuses made of jewels. And then like swooping over the lunar desert, this mythical blind bird, you can see its blind lonely eyes, and it's not called anything the bird, it's pure fantasy, but if it was called something it would be like – the long-beaked –

TRACKY. Loanshark.

SUSAN. You're on another planet you. You're on earth or some place.

TRACKY. Tex O'Donnell. East End Loans Limited. My Da's in debt to loansharks.

Pause.

SUSAN. Oh god. Poor Tex. Because violence isn't in his nature, Tracky.

SAMMY has entered. He's bought some 'lucky number' lottery tickets, and he's busy scouring the tickets with a ten pence piece.

SAMMY. You two. I thought something had blotted out the sun. Haw. No no, you won't get to me today. Happy happy happy. I'm so happy I'll likely have a heart-attack. I left Lucy on her own for a moment . . . phoning the Lord Provost's office.

SUSAN. Oh Mr Doak: I can't tell you!

SAMMY (*modestly, shrugging it off*). Modest: what did I do? (I'm just grateful to be alive.) Because I've answered my critics today.

LUCY comes on, with cellnet.

LUCY. Right: –

SAMMY. Were they helpful?

LUCY. I finally managed to squeeze a comment out of them. I can't believe these people, you'd think they'd love this story. Can we go?

She doesn't wait for him.

SAMMY. I generally like to round things off here with –

LUCY's gone.

(One of my best jokes is here.) Next stop: the world-famous Burrell Collection.

He exits after her.
Silence.

SUSAN. He's so happy I could cry.

TRACKY. That's what he's always like. I just switch off.

TRACKY goes.

SUSAN. Where are you going?

TRACKY. The Burrell.

She's gone. SUSAN on her own. Then – as the scene changes round about her –

SUSAN. Because I hope you don't blame me for this. – You're so insensitive, Tracky, I'm all mixed up in the middle of this and you just walk away.

Then she exits.

Scene Four

The Burrell Collection. On one wall are some Persian prayer rugs. In front of them, a long long black 'seat'. Also on display is an Etruscan pitcher.
TEX *enters with toolbox. Exits again.*
Enter AGNES DOAK. *She's still young, thirty-six, and when she can be bothered she cares about how she looks, or worries about how she looks. Considering she's come from her work, and considering she went to her work in an alcoholic blackout, she looks good. The initial impression – clothes and accessories – is of individuality – interesting splashes of colour – though a keener eye might see that this effect is partly accidental. The second impression is that of a worrier. The way she seems to be carrying too much stuff, coat, bag, shopping etc. And as she anxiously checks her appearance, she notices a scorch mark on her new good cream-coloured coat which she's never seen before. Just when she's got herself presentable, she panics. Drink. Into the shoulder-bag, out with a wee quarter bottle of whisky, takes a ladylike mouthful, then another, and puts it back.*
SUSAN *enters.*

SUSAN. Mrs Doak. It's me. Tracky's pal. Susan.

AGNES. Susan. Oh I never recognised you, darlin'. Susan?

SUSAN. Oh Mrs Doak, I can't tell you how I feel! I don't think
    Tracky approves but (Tracky!): she's not very in touch with her
    feelings. Because he's utterly gorgeous. And he really like *listens*
    to me, which is, because you know what men are like: they
    listen to you for about fifteen seconds and then they think
    you're dead self-centred.

AGNES. Susan?

SUSAN. Susan MacAlindon. I saw you last Saturday. Remember?
    That was the night you set yourself on fire.

AGNES (*mildly indignant*). Nobody mentioned that to me.

SUSAN. I smothered the flames with your new good coat.

AGNES. Oh well . . . I won't hold it against you. (Use an old
    blanket next time, will you, pet.) – It's Sammy I'm looking for,
    have you seen him?

SUSAN. You're pure voodoo, Mrs Doak, how did you know Mr
    Doak was here?

AGNES. I phoned him.

SUSAN. Aw.

AGNES. Has he fallen out with me? I had a wee night last night – *Tracky*'s pal, of course I know you! (what am I thinking about?) – and when I woke up this morning I was at my work (Belvidere Hospital?) What a fright I got, waking up with my plastic gloves on! – and I must've been hard at it because the toilet pan was shining.

TRACKY *enters*.

TRACKY. Mammy! Susan! What are you doing here?

AGNES. I've come to make it up with your Da. Will you be in for your tea, darlin'? I got some chinky ribs out the butcher's, your favourite.

TRACKY. Give the drink a chuck, Ma, will you?

AGNES. I will, darlin'. I have. That's what I came to tell your Da. I've stopped. No way: this carry-on?: and a memory like a ditch . . . no idea what . . .

TRACKY (*to* SUSAN). If you're looking for Tex, I just seen him with a toolbox. Oh don't worry – I didn't talk to him.

SUSAN. It's not what you think, Tracky. What's so bad about that, I only want to bring two people together – she's got contacts in the music biz so think twice before you go and judge people because what about the time you lumbered me with Mongo Robertson –

AGNES. (School), do they not teach you join your sentences up?

SUSAN. – and then Mongo called me a lezzy.

AGNES. It's like a pile-up on the motorway.

SUSAN. – just because he tastes like antiseptic? – So *that's* why I'm going. (*i.e. 'this explains my exit to look for* TEX'. *And she exits.*)

AGNES. Barbecue sauce. You like that, don't you.

TRACKY. Oh Mammy.

AGNES. It's you I get it for.

TRACKY. Did I used to be *nice*? Likes of, when I was wee. Was I nice then?

AGNES. What kinna question's that? All wee girls are nice.

TRACKY. Tell me then.

AGNES. Tell you what?

TRACKY. Tell me . . . (about me.)

AGNES. . . . (about you) . . .

You used to have a lovely pink all-in-one babysuit, I remember that. (Is that what you mean?) You were a wee doll. They say all wee girls suit pink of course, but then you had the fair hair too.

TRACKY. That's a lie! – did I?

AGNES. Yes! – did you not know that? – Then when you got up a bit, when we ever went our holidays, you were a terrible terrible thoughtful wee girl – is that the time? – soon as you got money first thing you thought was to get your Daddy a present. Oh you loved your Daddy! Every day for a fortnight, we'd lie back on the beach and you'd go off and come back with something else.

TRACKY. What like?

AGNES. Oh for goodness sake, Tracky . . . a lot of rubbish likely, you were only eight. – How did you, sleep OK last night?

Beat.

TRACKY. See if my Daddy asks you for money, don't give him it, right? Because he's got to face facts.

AGNES. What facts?

TRACKY. Just. He wants to think everything always turns out good in the end. Well it doesn't.

TRACKY *goes, leaving* AGNES *mystified.*

AGNES. They baffle you, don't they?

And AGNES *goes.*

SAMMY *and* LUCY *come on.* LUCY *has a look at the prayer rugs.* SAMMY *stays close to the exit and keeps a lookout for* TEX.

SAMMY. Because to tell you the truth, I could do with a bit of luck.

When did they say they'd get back to you?

I suppose you can't blame them. It's a big story you're giving them. Though as you say, what's big about it? But to *them* it's big. A wee local newspaper like them?

LUCY *has wandered over to look at the pitcher. Glances down at the card that tells you what it is.*

I see you're like me – no, carry on, don't let me break your concentration! – You're like me. You like to look right deep into things. Will I tell you the actual real significance of that?

LUCY. It says. It's Etruscan.

SAMMY. Someone with your training? – you can see through that.

LUCY (*incredible irritation: incredibly repressed*). What.

SAMMY. Do I have to *tell* you? Because (tell *you*?): infrastructure.

He leaves a pause for effect. Then explains.

This is the Burrell Collection, correct? So there's Assyrian tools, Mesopotamian artefacts, Rodin sculptures, Dégas ballerinas. What's that got to do with Glasgow; nothing – right? Wrong. Look beyond that artefact you've got eight thousand hotel beds; international airport; permanent art facilities; plus a big new thingwy centre. So. Do you get it now? That thing there is the symbol of a city that can deliver a tourism strategy!! As well as which –

He's looking around for TEX.

– luck? If someone flung a sweetie at me now and again.

TRACKY *arrives.*

TRACKY. Da! Lend us twenty notes, will you?

SAMMY. I know to look at me – Mr Happy, right? But I can be sad too.

TRACKY. I want to go to the Gift Shop.

SAMMY. That's what the government *should* ban. School holidays. Any kids yourself, Lucy?

LUCY. Not in this country.

SAMMY. Take my advice: you try to spoil them and you only end up ruining them.

TRACKY. It's a present for you I want. They've got these models: one's a Glasgow tenement and one's a Provand's Lordship, what one d'you want most?

LUCY. Oh, is it your birthday?

SAMMY. (Luck? – if –

LUCY. I've given up presents. I cut my parents off.

TRACKY. I used to always buy him presents.

SAMMY. – if someone flung a sweet at me . . .) So you did – so
she did, I'd forgotten that! Oh she loved her Daddy! There was
a time – presents for her Daddy? – she couldn't stop.

TRACKY. So big joke!

SAMMY. Presents one thing but this was desperate. – There was
this once, abroad somewhere, she got me a butter dish. So that
was another argument. Her mother's like that: a butter dish?
So I'm like that: aye a butter dish! She goes: why a butter dish?
So I goes: because you smashed the one we had off the wall!
Aye *did* I, she goes. That's the standard of what you get from
her: aye *did* I. So that's when I chucked it, argue with that? Aye
you *did*, I goes!

TRACKY. It was only a stupid wee butter dish.

SAMMY. *Word for Word* I remember that: that's verbatim. –
Butter dish: lovely delicate-looking and (like crystal) thing.

LUCY. I just send a Xmas card to the budgie now.

TRACKY. So go on, Da: twenty notes: don't be miserable. For
the good times.

The pressure on SAMMY.

SAMMY. Twenty notes?

TRACKY. You're a pal.

SAMMY. I haven't got twenty notes. Haw. (Came out in the
wrong jacket this morning.)

He's wearing a T-shirt.

TRACKY. Oh god.

SAMMY. I don't have two pounds. I've got one pound seventy-
eight ten eleven pee.

TRACKY. That's tragic.

SAMMY. Ho – 'tragic'.

TRACKY. I know. How're you going to pay the man with the
hammer drill?

SAMMY. (Man with the . . .)

TRACKY. Toolbox. Because if he doesn't get a hunner notes off you he's into your brickwork with his masonry attachment.

Beat – SAMMY trying to keep his front – then –

SAMMY. I'm not paying for shelves I didn't order! Simple as that, Lucy. A joiner can't just walk into your house and put up a complete integrated wall-system *and expect to get away with it.*

TEX enters. He's carrying a red steel toolbox.

TEX. Mr Glasgow.

SAMMY. I didn't even like the colour.

TEX smiles. Crosses the room and places the toolbox somewhere conspicuous. He places it with great care.

TEX. So, Mr Glasgow – imagine knocking into you, with my tools.

SAMMY is anxious LUCY shouldn't connect this apparition with the hammer drill man, so –

SAMMY. Listen to him being formal too. 'Mr Glasgow'. Good to see you too, my friend. Can I introduce you to Lucy, journalist friend of mine. Watch it: she can see right through you.

TEX. How, what's there to see? – So I'm baffled: how did I know you'd be here?

SAMMY. Aw heah: you're at the kidding now.

TEX. *I'm* at the kidding.

SAMMY. He's at the kidding. This is a business pal of mine.

TEX. *I'm* not at the kidding.

SAMMY. Well who's kidding who here? Someone's kidding.

TRACKY. Are you keeping up with them, Lucy?

SAMMY. She's a journalist this one. How did you know I was here? You saw my taxi.

TEX. Put it this way. That's one explanation.

SAMMY. Did you *see* my taxi? Some coat on her: like a seal. That's what I was saying to them earlier, that's what I was saying to you earlier: she's got a coat on her like a seal.

TEX. Seal? Do you want me to go out there and club it?

SAMMY. See the wee ironic smile there. We talk the same language me and him. Banks? – away and eff that. I'd already bought my taxi, all I wanted: some cash to clear my debt and get me started. Petrol money. That's an expression, Lucy: 'petrol money'. That's what gets you started. Then luck: I bump into this crazy bastard here.

TEX. Not me.

SAMMY. 'Not you'? Haw: not him, he says. He's quite correct (I met the pedantic bastard later) met some other guy first. But same company, am I right? Same company.

TRACKY. Just as well you came, Tex.

SAMMY. . . . Tex . . . ?

TRACKY. You're just in time. Some mad bastard of a joiner is after him with a hammer drill.

The toolbox.

SAMMY. Will you stop saying that?! You've got this young lady terrorised.

LUCY (*unfazed*). I'm quite curious actually, I enjoy danger. When you've travelled with a trainload of Millwall supporters in their prime . . . It was a piece I was doing for some German magazine. I sold it as The Inner Life of the English Football Hooligan. – The train was fine once a bloke called Andy with a swastika on his forehead took me under his wing. But then we got attacked in a pub by some Leeds United scum.

TEX. Bad?

LUCY. Oh – I tell you. I tell you. Sixteen people were killed. It was terrible. Terrible.

An awful embarrassed silence. The phone goes. LUCY *answers it.*

LUCY. Yes . . . speaking . . . not at all, not at all . . .

TEX. Sixteen dead?

LUCY. . . . yes, of course . . .

TEX. Sixteen?

SAMMY. She landed lucky that day. Front page.

LUCY. . . . so you want me to . . .

TEX. I don't recall reading that? Do you recall reading that?

LUCY. . . . fine . . . no-no . . . yes – could you give me five minutes? – five minutes and I'll phone the copy in. Fine . . . bye . . . yes bye . . . bye bye.

LUCY *closes the aerial and looks in her bag for her copy. Nervous, excited and distracted.*

They're going with the story for the afternoon edition.

SAMMY *makes inarticulate noises of delight.*

I have to – where's my copy? – excuse me while I – have to phone my copy in.

And she goes.

SAMMY. Danny Glasgow, one of the city's flourishing tour-operators and a city institution today said. Up yer bakey the lot of you! (Apart from you, Tex: you believed in me.) Mad? – me? – *I'm* mad? Well not according to the papers. Not according to the *Evening Times*.

And SAMMY *makes to exit!*

TEX. Are you going somewhere, son?

SAMMY *stops in his tracks.*

I make it two hundred and seventy-five notes you owe us. What do you make it?

SAMMY. Two hundred and seventy-five?

TEX. Good. We're agreed then. We'll call that sixty quid a week for five weeks – fair? – first instalment due after I've sauntered down to the cafeteria for a coffee and sauntered back.

TEX *saunters off, leaving the toolbox. Pause.*

TRACKY. I used to – likes of –

SAMMY. Crisis? What crisis?

TRACKY. More than I liked her.

SAMMY. 'Twenty notes'! (Brain 'flu.)

TRACKY. More than I loved my Mammy.

SAMMY. Judgement? I run my hand through my hair and I cut my finger. Millions of shitty wee bits of glass in my hair.

He exits.

TRACKY. You were a pal.

She exits.

AGNES *comes on, harassed, followed by* SUSAN.

AGNES. Where the hell has Sammy got to? See this place.

SUSAN. So do you see now?

AGNES. Will you let me get a seat, Susan.

SUSAN. Oh god. I wish my love life wasn't so complicated.

AGNES (*anger*). And don't crowd me!

SUSAN's *miles away.* AGNES *has sat on the seat with her back to* SUSAN *and is now scrabbling in her bag, looking for something.*

I get enough of that in bed.

SUSAN. I thought you and him slept in separate rooms.

AGNES *has got her whisky out: she takes a secretive sip.*

AGNES. I still wake up sweating, don't I? – So tell me again. This fella you fancy used to go out with our Tracky.

SUSAN. No! I told you: he was somebody's pal, came up to us at the dancing, said he'd got these tickets for the Onslaught gig. We hardly knew him. So we're in the pub before the gig and he gives Tracky an eternity ring, like right in front of all his pals? They're all slagging him, but just because he's not afraid to show his feelings. So he phones her up the next day and asks her out, just the two of them.

AGNES. So she went out with him.

SUSAN. No! She told him she had a sick mother to clean up – know how, to put him off? – and she'd to stay in every night for a fortnight That's when he asked for his eternity ring back. So it's like – she's missed her chance.

SAMMY *enters, sees* SUSAN *and goes for her.*

SAMMY. Susan. Cash. Never mind the blank expressions – quick.

SUSAN. I've no money on me, Mr Doak.

SAMMY. You put your hands in your pockets very fast.

AGNES. Sammy. What is it, what's the matter?

SAMMY. *Rustle* (oh wonderful: my spouse: my helpmate) empty those pockets before my eardrums burst!

As SUSAN pulls about eighteen Twix wrappers out of her pocket –

AGNES. Sammy – this might be the wrong time –

SAMMY. Haw!

AGNES. – but I came to say sorry about last night. (What did I do?)

SAMMY. Eighteen Twix wrappers.

SUSAN. I'm vegetarian, Mr Doak.

AGNES. Fair enough, wrong time, I won't push it. (I've chucked the drink.)

SAMMY. Cash I want, not sweety papers! *I'm in a predicament here.* I've got a loanshark at my back wanting sixty notes *out my skin.*

Points at AGNES.

No thanks to you.

AGNES. Did you not get a fare today?

SAMMY. Look, Agnes: you've said sorry, we've made up, now don't start right away making a mess again.

AGNES. Because that's fifty quid on your tail for starters.

SAMMY. See! That's you got the whole thing confused from the outset. No wonder my judgement's – : you *poking my brains* night and day.

SUSAN. I don't understand, Mr Doak. The loan people must've gave you a warning.

SAMMY. A warn- . . . eh?

SUSAN. Because if you push them too far, what do you expect?

AGNES. You told me on the phone you had a fare.

SAMMY. I don't have the language for you two. What do you define a warning as, Sweety Wrappers. (Some bloke came up to me in the pub and had a polite friendly word in my ear.) Then I go home and find my wife is ablaze. (I can't remember everything.)

LUCY enters.

LUCY. Well done, well done! I honestly think we should take this further. What do you think, why don't we look at potential sites?

AGNES. So you have got a fare.

SAMMY. Yes I've got a fare.

AGNES. Oh I see. It's like that, is it?

LUCY. What? Because that's one thing I *don't* do. I only have sex in emergencies. – Is that what you meant?

SAMMY. So what'll we call it so far, Lucy? Fifty's the usual . . . plus the usual something on top for the driver, which is just: 'on top' money we call it.

LUCY. But I thought –

SAMMY. Because why think the worst? That's (*my* opinion) that's the curse afflicts us all: pecks our eyes out.

LUCY. Sorry?

SAMMY. Sorry? If you've got it, flaunt it: that's what I say. (Plus the use of the phone) for*get* the phone for*get* the phone, the phone's another way of saying – . – Nothing against you being English. Different people show their appreciation different ways. A tribe in Africa I read about shows its appreciation: I'm talking anthropology here: this tribe, someone wants to show their appreciation they do it, a different way entirely . . . whereas we've got 'on top' money. Different customs. – (Can you make it cash?) Not that business isn't good, business is good, it's my personal life that's really bad.

SUSAN. They're called The Evil Doers.

SAMMY. To tell you the truth, Lucy . . .

SUSAN. It's up to you but this could make you in the music biz.

SAMMY. . . . this is my wife here . . .

SUSAN (*taking the huff at* LUCY's *perceived lack of response*). Fine! OK then, but talent? Because forget it: it's gone.

SUSAN *storms off.*

SAMMY. . . . wife here . . . she'd admit it herself actually – no fault of her own, more bad communication than anything. The point being (you'll laugh) it was actually her got the joiner in.

You'd admit that yourself, wouldn't you, Agnes? No fault of her own but she's dropped me in a quagmire.

AGNES. Has someone left their toolbox?

SAMMY. A quarry.

LUCY. I hate this. I'm sorry but I hate this. You offered me a free ride. Now you're trying to steam money out of me. If I'd thought you were going to embarrass me, I wouldn't have come, would I?

AGNES. I'm sitting here looking at it too.

TEX *enters*.

TEX. Samuel, Samuel. That's the second time I've called your name.

LUCY (*still brittle*). I could write you a cheque if that's any use.

TEX. Time to collect.

LUCY. Write a cheque for what, ten?

AGNES. You could *use* some tools, Sammy – could you not? Wait and I'll see what's there.

SAMMY'*s spinning from one to the other: speechless: reduced temporarily to inarticulate noises: as* AGNES *goes to investigate the toolbox.*

SAMMY. Agnes, would you not poke – enjoy your coffee, Tex? – tell you what, I'll fling in the phone and call it thirty – Agnes! – that could be a radio-controlled bomb for all you know.

And in his terror he points at TEX; *who smiles, hand in pocket.*

So will you – because those things are more sensitive than you are!

AGNES. It's just tools.

SAMMY. *Of course* tools! It's a toolbox, what did you expect, Pandora's box?

LUCY *hands* SAMMY *a cheque.*

LUCY. Cheque. Thirty pounds.

SAMMY. Fine – well played, well played – any cash on you?

LUCY. You exchange *that* for cash.

SAMMY. Excellent.

He hands her the cheque back and holds out his hand.

Thirty quid.

LUCY. Nobody pays *me* cash. – I don't *have* any cash. – I don't use it.

SAMMY. Then could you cash a cheque at the Gift Shop? *I'm in a labyrinth here!*

SUSAN *and* TRACKY *enter from different directions.*

SUSAN. Tex – I've been looking all over for you.

LUCY (*brittle*). I get very inflexible when I'm shouted at.

SUSAN (*to* TEX). Ignore *her*: she wouldn't know talent if it spat in her face.

SAMMY. Inflexible? I'll tell you what's inflexible –

SUSAN. So listen:

SAMMY. – a golf club.

SUSAN. I fancy you, right?

SAMMY. A three iron right in the gob.

SUSAN. Right? So relax, you're all tense: I might be a crossbred mean-scene crazyhead rocket queen but I'm still a dead nice person.

SAMMY. Right in the teeth.

SUSAN. I know you're married and what you do for a living –

SAMMY. Compared to a golf club, teeth are pragmatic.

SUSAN. – but I think if you love someone you shouldn't try and change them otherwise it's not love.

AGNES. I see. So you're – him. You're Susan's –

SAMMY. Agnes! Will you stop listening to the life-form in the leather jacket!

AGNES. You're Susan's –

SAMMY. Concentration's not her strong point. Agnes – I'm discussing my teeth here.

AGNES. That's –. I see: Susan's –. And I thought you were the loanshark, the one that's out to get Sammy?

SAMMY. *Because who'll pay for the dental work I'll need?*

LUCY. A loanshark. I see! I thought you were a joiner.

SAMMY. How did – ? Who told her? Was that you, Agnes?

SUSAN. (Otherwise it's not love.)

SAMMY. Oh well: exposed: wonderful. We can all relax now.

LUCY. I see! – Oh well, I'd better try the Gift Shop, hadn't I? I don't mind paying cash if I know it's going to be laundered.

And off she goes.

SAMMY. Half way there, Tex. Thirty notes, will that do you? Say I flung in my . . . (phone).

TEX. Come on away, son. I'll take you for a drive. I've been as fair as I can be. Now I have to be fair to myself.

SUSAN. Oh god! I'm going to cry.

SAMMY. I'm too reasonable, that's my problem: I hurt myself. Start a small business in the city and everyone's against you – (apart from you, Tex, you believed in me) – the whole mentality's against you!

TEX. That's your time.

TEX *motions* SAMMY *out.* SAMMY *starts to walk.*

AGNES. And you wouldn't think to ask me for the money?

SAMMY *stops.*

I'm too low-class or something? I'm too rubbish? You might as well come right out and say it, Sammy, it's that bloody obvious. I'm the only one you *haven't* pestered.

SAMMY. I never knew you had any money.

AGNES. What's he been saying about me, has he told you a lot of lies? I work for the biggest employer in the country!

SAMMY. Thirty quid?

AGNES. Yes! See how much he thinks of me – this is the day my wages go into the bank. All I have to do is go home and find my cashcard.

SUSAN. Oh Tex.

TEX. I shouldn't even contemplate it to be truthful. But right –
to show you I'm a Labour man – fair enough.

SUSAN. Oh god! I'm going to cry.

TEX. I'm a soft bastard. So right, I'll say this once. How you get
the money's your problem: I want you outside the Wimpey in
Ingram Street, seven o'clock, with ninety quid in your paws.
Ninety quid for the next three weeks, right? (Three weeks of
this psychology is all I can take.) Ninety. Ingram Street. Seven.

He exits.

SUSAN. So don't be surprised, he's a family man. He's got a wee
boy called Christopher, of course he's got feelings.

TRACKY. See this family: one of these days I am going to snap.

*She exits, and SUSAN goes after her, leaving SAMMY and AGNES
alone for the first time. Terrible silence as they search for something to
say to each other. But they only have one thing in common: mutual
guilt.*

SAMMY (*benevolent despair*). Tracky. Haw.

AGNES. One thing anyway, she'll break a few hearts.

SAMMY. Like her mother.

AGNES. The boys are queueing up for her.

SAMMY. Like her mother.

Beat.

AGNES. Ahch: it's too late now. She never grew up the way *I*
wanted.

SAMMY. She never grew up the way *I* wanted either.

AGNES. And her name's Attracta! Attracta!

SAMMY. She can be cheeky too right enough.

AGNES. Ahch – Sa – : just! –

SAMMY. What?

AGNES. You talk that much rubbish, so you do. If you'd been
firm with her when she was younger. Discipline? – that was my
domain. Then when I did give her the odd clout all she had to
do was run to you and you'd take her to a match or something.

SAMMY. (Match.)

AGNES. Oh don't kid yourself, you can forget, you're stupid that way, but I can't.

SAMMY (*moved*). Scotland–Spain. She saw one of the greats that night: Kenny. Takes a ball off Cooper, comes in from the right, saunters across their penalty-box past about three of them, then left foot: immaculate: 3–1. – She'll remember that night, seven years old or not. Kenny was . . . Kenny!

LUCY *returns.*

LUCY. They were very friendly – where is everyone? Where's our friend? The young loanshark.

SAMMY. The danger was averted, last minute.

LUCY. Oh. I got the thirty pounds. – Oh well never mind. Shall we go then? I want to get this piece wrapped up earlyish so I can sort out accommodation etcetera.

She goes. Slight pause, then SAMMY *follows her. But before he exits –*

SAMMY. Did I tell you? I'm in this afternoon's paper?

AGNES. Paper. What as?

SAMMY. Danny Glasgow!

He exits.

AGNES. Oh Sammy, that's great. The paper? Wait till I show them at my work – does she tell them what your real name is?

She gets herself ready to go.

– show them at my work. Ahch why not – Margaret's always bumming on about her scientist daughter that burns wee guinea-pigs up at the Royal. All so as she can write it up for her Ph.D.? Well we've got more to say for ourselves than guinea-pigs. Eh Sammy? So don't run away and leave me.

As she goes, she stops for a sip of whisky.

Margaret: she *is* a guinea-pig: squeak squeak squeak: I'd like to burn her, see how she likes it.

Exit.

ACT TWO

Scene One

Waste ground. An abandoned pram. Dead football. SAMMY *and* LUCY *enter stage right. Both have a copy of the* Evening Times. SAMMY *is low-key, distracted.*

LUCY. Well this is absolutely right, isn't it? Big empty space.

SAMMY. Yes.

LUCY (*congratulatory*). I mean! This is almost the city centre.

SAMMY. I keep saying. We really have a lot to offer; (land-developers).

LUCY. How big is it?

SAMMY. Big empty space: could be any distance. Like a factory exterior, walk from one end to the other, nothing to look at but corrugated iron, you run out of (things to say to yourself).

SAMMY *looks off stage right. Worried about* AGNES.

Walk to the middle: get its scale. I'll stay here and give you something to judge by.

LUCY. Fine. Then I'll let you and your wife get on and find a cash-mashine.

She goes.

SAMMY. Open-space area? – her brain.

SAMMY *looks at his watch, looks off at* AGNES.

Agnes. (Whatever it was happened passed me by.) Agnes, will you –

He covers his face as if AGNES *has just fallen.*

– (stay on your feet?) What chance has an *economy* got? There's another hold-up, now it's her tights. Patience, Sammy son, patience: think of the souls in limbo. Because that's what she wants, she wants to – tights? – (tear my *face* off).

AGNES comes on, stage right, tights torn, dragging her coat along the ground. She's very drunk, but she's still keeping it together physically . . . it's her psychology we see, the sudden shifts in mood . . .
She hurries on blind, with a copy of the Evening Times, *stops short when she sees SAMMY.*

AGNES. Oh. You. It's well seen I've got money. Oh don't kid yourself, you're all swarming round me now.

She sits on the ash ground, possibly putting her shoulderbag under her.

Money money money, brought me nothing but misery: and look at my tights now!

SAMMY (*concerned*). Did you hurt yourself?

AGNES (*as if in reply*). Ah dry your eyes, you'll get your money! Money – if I had my way I'd *give* it away, every last miserable penny.

SAMMY. Have I mentioned money once? Have I?

AGNES. *Yes* money! (You put everyone to that much trouble) – money? – you don't even mention it to your fares.

SAMMY. Oh no: back away, Sammy: don't involve yourself.

AGNES. You even married me for my money. Oh don't kid yourself: my Mammy might have been a single parent but she never swore. Not like the ones you get nowadays.

SAMMY. I've seen you manufacture a fight before.

AGNES. Did I say she wasn't? Did I? So she was a dinner-lady! *She was a good decent woman.* (Ho. I must take after my father –

SAMMY. – swamp – where do you start?

AGNES. – him that effed off and left us.)

SAMMY. So forget an argument. I'm out.

Beat. For AGNES to glance at him, appraise the situation.

AGNES. Ho. Because you know you'd lose.

SAMMY. Correct I'd lose, I *know* I'd lose.

AGNES. You're fuck'n' right you would.

SAMMY. I know that.

AGNES. You're fuck'n' right you know that. So just don't argue with me, (I'm not in the mood).

AGNES *looks out front, sees the sun going down, in all its glory, and is suddenly seized with almost religious awe.*

AGNES. Oh god (glory . . .)

SAMMY. Sun starting to go down now.

AGNES. See that.

SAMMY. (Time.)

AGNES. Eye-shadow clouds: and flame-orange . . . like a young girl with her make-up on.

SAMMY. For a (night out at the dancing.) See the time!

SUSAN *and* TRACKY *come on, each with their copy of the* Evening Times. TRACKY's *also got fags and a bottle of something (alcohol) out of the offy. She's been sent there by her Mammy.*

AGNES. There's my fags now: hip hip! Twenty Lambert and Butler, did you get them OK?

TRACKY. Yeah.

TRACKY *shows the fags. She overdoes this gesture, and at the same time attempts to underplay the bottle at her side.* SAMMY *and* AGNES *are also very aware of the unmentioned bottle.*

AGNES. And are you going to smoke them for me? Bring them over here to me, darlin', or your Da will –. Non-smokers?, they don't believe in cancer.

As TRACKY *crosses,* SUSAN *surveys the open space area;* SAMMY *keeps his eye on the bottle.*

SUSAN. EMI. Imagine it.

SAMMY. (Cancer.)

AGNES *takes the fags and – fast – the bottle, which she puts under or in her bag.*

SUSAN. Is this where she's saying it'll be?

SAMMY. Times like this I could cry. (Glorious summer's evening.)

His concentration is on AGNES.

SUSAN. Because this is ideal.

SAMMY. (Nobody paying a blind bit of notice.)

AGNES. 'EMI'. There's always something supposed to be coming. Jobs? – ahch, they've been trying to run an economy for years, pet. It's time we started our own. Scotland. Get our independence and apply to join a united Germany.

SAMMY. Is that – ? What hope – ? Because – ahhhhhhhhhhhhhhhhg!

He does this at AGNES, an attack, which genuinely disturbs her.

AGNES. *For crying out – ! Sammy!* I'm not even going to answer him, because you watch and learn, Tracky. My mother detested loudness too.

SAMMY. 'Scotland'.

AGNES. Anybody raised their voice to her and she just waltzed-out-that-room. 'Just leave them in hell', she used to say. Here Tracky, here's something for getting me my fags.

And she goes into her purse and gets out a tenner.

Here.

She holds it out to her.

TRACKY. A tenner?

AGNES. Yes!: look at that sky: you young girls should be all dolled up and – what? Away to the dancing and do some damage amongst the fellas. Use them before they use you, you use them first.

TRACKY *reaches for the tenner, reluctant, embarrassed. AGNES suddenly grabs her wrist and holds her, though not too harshly.*

Here. Here. Do you love me?

TRACKY (*uncomfortable*). Oh Mammy.

AGNES. (What's wrong, is my lipstick smudged?) Do you love me?

TRACKY. You don't have to give me money.

AGNES. Ohff! Don't *you* start on about money.

SAMMY. What chance has an economy got?

AGNES. I'm asking you a question. Because I know –. I can be an old witch at times. Sure I am? I am. I know that. A horrible old witch.

AGNES *touches* TRACKY's *face, desperate for love.*

But oh: see the feelings I get. The feelings I get.

TRACKY (*moved*). Oh Mammy.

AGNES. When I'm alone and I can't take any more. And I look at myself . . . oh don't think I don't know . . . I look at myself and (ahch: shhh . . .) mother? Mothers bake! Mothers sew things! Ahch . . . I'm sorry, Tracky, but see mother, that's just the age I am. Inside I'm your age.

Slight pause.

TRACKY. I tell everyone I love you, don't I, Susan? – I love you.

She means this. But there's something exaggerated and desperate about it as well. As if she's feeling the feeling she ought to feel.

SUSAN. She tells everyone, Mrs Doak. All about how young you are and how much you're a feminist – likes of the way you don't take any crap –

TRACKY. (Shut up, Susan.)

SUSAN. – anybody tries to use you, you use them first, and like make a mess, let *them* clear it up and I agree: nobody complains when a *man* looks stupid in public –

AGNES. Ohff!

TRACKY. That *is not* what I said.

AGNES. Because I knew that living-room carpet off by heart. If that's *feminism!*

TRACKY. I didn't say you were a *feminist,* I said. I said you were a feminist but I didn't say. I don't even want to discuss it. Why is everything a laugh in this family? We discuss Scotland and that's a laugh. Then we discuss feminism and that's another laugh – and *I don't want a tenner!*

She throws the tenner back at AGNES.

AGNES. Ho. Here's another one raises her voice.

SAMMY. 'Scotland'. I was discussing Scotland. Her – ask your mother a reasonable question and she chips a tarantula at you. How can you discuss –

AGNES. You can discuss things without raising your voice, Tracky.

SAMMY. You can't discuss nothing with a tarantula in your hair.

TRACKY. (I do something good comes out bad, say something good comes out – stupid.) It's time someone got a grip on this family!

SAMMY. Who? You?

TRACKY. What's funny about that? You should see what I'm looking at.

AGNES. Oh let her go, Sammy. I've no time for that. (Save the family?) What's she inferring?

TRACKY *has crossed to the abandoned pram and now starts to push it towards the exit.*

SAMMY. The only thing that'll save this family –

AGNES. 'Family'. Ho.

SAMMY. – save this family is a fatal car-smash! Killing the lot of us!

TRACKY'*s gone.*

AGNES. (Pram . . . ?)

SUSAN. I know. She's unreal. I better go after her. And listen Mr Doak: I think it's terrible you're only on page seven. I mean: EMI. I know it's only a rumour but page one's only a rumour too. Look: two thousand jobs to go *question mark.*

SUSAN *exits.*

AGNES. (Pram . . . ?)

SAMMY. Give us a swally (swig).

AGNES. *What* drink? Oh that.

She gets out her bottle, hands it to SAMMY.

Ah why not: half six: relax: you've done your bit for today: sit here and watch the sunset.

SAMMY. (Sunset.)

AGNES. I could look at that for hours.

SAMMY *sits.*

SAMMY. We better go get Lucy: find a cash-machine.

AGNES. Oh there she's waving.

AGNES *waves back at* LUCY, *hypocritically.*

AGNES. You used to be a *good* judge of character. You used to
pride yourself. Mind (before my Mammy died and we got her
house off the Council) I got us the flat in Eldon Street. Joe
Brady and that other one –

SAMMY. Mick.

AGNES. I thought they were friendly big fellas but you were
suspicious from the start.

SAMMY. Jealousy had nothing to do with it, Agnes. They were
dope-heads.

AGNES. They were nice enough to me.

SAMMY. Skins and scales and –

AGNES. Aw, where's your sense of adventure? And then the
English girl with the whispery voice that looked like a ghost.

SAMMY. Debbie.

AGNES. You remember *her.*

SAMMY. Debbie? She was an experience.

As he goes on, he begins to enjoy re-discovering this weird episode in his
and AGNES' *shared past . . .*

Sat there all night with her Russian hat on, smoking dope and
not saying a word. Then about five in the morning once you'd
crashed out on the floor she'd start talking about the gods. I'd
sit there nodding profoundly – all about some gods liked her
and some hated her – and two hours later she'd start to get
annoyed at me. All I did was sit there and nod and she'd get
annoyed at me . . . go to her bed.

AGNES. So Liam and Mick arrive back one afternoon with a
pram they've stolen for me outside a chemist's

SAMMY. mental cases

AGNES. to make up for the night before when they came back at
four in the morning

SAMMY. on speed

AGNES. from the guru who wasn't a guru and told them not to

worship *anyone* so they rip all their posters down and you
smack Liam in the mouth because he wants Debbie to take
down her poster of Stalin and you believe in free speech that
night and Debbie only ever done up about two buttons on her
cheesecloth

SAMMY. Stalin . . . that was to make up for her lack of
confidence, of course.

AGNES. so you get a sore face off Mick and next day they give
me a nearly-new pram to compensate. – I don't know why they
thought of a pram.

SAMMY (*'explanation'*). Head-cases.

AGNES. I wasn't pregnant. I wasn't planning on it either. So why
on earth?

SAMMY. Eh?

Because they thought we were ordinary. (That's why.) They
thought we should settle down.

*And the moment of communion between them is over. Back to the big
empty space.*

AGNES. *We* were ordinary? They were from *Fife*.

SAMMY. Twenty to. Come on we'll get Lucy.

SAMMY *exits stage left.*
Beat.
SAMMY *re-enters in a hurry.*

SAMMY. Quick.

AGNES. What is it?

SAMMY. Lucy saw them. That's what she was trying to tell us.
That wee bag a' rats has taken the wheels off my taxi.

LUCY *enters as* SAMMY *exits, and* AGNES *gets to her feet.*

LUCY (*as she crosses*). I don't even know where we are.

She exits after SAMMY.

AGNES. Oh leave me! And what does this mean, do we have to
walk? – Sammy! Sammy! – This family! Am I the only one of
you that can *keep still* for more than five minutes? – Ahcch, to
hell.

AGNES *exits.*

Scene Two

Another bit of waste ground. TRACKY *comes on pushing pram on top of which are two big wheels.* SUSAN *trundles on after her.*

SUSAN. Because that's what it's all about: hell and confusion: and like battling against an unseen foe? We could make a brilliant album of it. Heavy heavy sounds, heavy dark bass, and millions of dry ice because it's like mystical as well. I mean: I wish *my* Mammy was something. Like if she was an alky or a paranoid schizophrenic at least she'd *be* something, instead of just a *sad*case.

TRACKY. Susan. Will you give me a hand with these wheels?

SUSAN. I honestly can't, Tracky. A doctor once told me not to lift anything too heavy or I might get a fallen womb. Oh god, I wish I wasn't so *complicated*. It's great the way you just get on with things, you're so *straightforward*.

TRACKY *turns the pram over. A gesture of frustration. She knows the wheels will solve nothing, and she's beginning to feel stupid.*

TRACKY. *Because he needs his feet cut off!* He thinks he can jump about here there everywhere, dance round town keeping everyone happy, it's time he stood still and *thought*.

Pause. The wheels.

SUSAN. What will you do with them now?

TRACKY. Something.

SUSAN. Burn them?

TRACKY. Because I'm the only one in the family with a – (sense). Him?

SUSAN. Because we're too old for that.

TRACKY. Him? – 'Did you sleep alright?' How could I sl-, cut off my ears and – bury them under the pillow?

SUSAN. This is like the time we ended up in Falkirk with the two wee Lebanese sailors, then ran away and left them.

TRACKY. Yes I listen. Of course I listen. Because if I didn't, because of course I do, crying, tears, fake tears, blah blah *making up*, making up's the worst: that's when you realise you're the only one in the family with a sense of responsibility.

TEX *enters. More hurried than usual. Very uptight.*

TEX. I question myself.

SUSAN. Tex.

TEX. I really begin to question myself. 'What am I doing?' – right? Am I trying to keep a family together? Because fuck. See when people ask me what I do (gets on your tits right enough), people ask me I say: me? – something like the St Vincent de Paul. I visit the poor; and I like to remain anonymous. But you people! – To give you another perspective: I'm watching you, right?: the whole family's surveying a piece of waste ground, twenty to seven, fine, no panic. Then scatter. All of a sudden scatter. *Did someone lob a grenade at you?* Then I get round; and you're stripping your father's one and only asset, then he comes after you –

TRACKY. Is he still coming after me?

TEX. – *then he chucks it!* (heads for, christ, Ingram Street) and I'm left there like that: family? – what family? – thin air. Then my car breaks down. – Am I communicating right? Can I introduce myself: *I am not a social worker.* – Fear. I say that, because no fear? – you're one emotion short. A normal family: they're all over the place, chaos, then *I* go and see them. And they've got a structure then, so fine so it's temporary *so is the universe: even the solar system isn't stable*, could fly off the handle at any moment and bastarding Jupiter: it's not even *solid*: volcanic gases or somefuck'n'thing . . . (chaos). Normal family, I go in there and give them a crisis and they're like that: they like it: because at least it's something . . . takes their mind off their other problems.

With no thought for the consequences on her future fertility, SUSAN *picks up a wheel.*

SUSAN. I'll help you take the tyres back, OK? So don't get upset. She just got all involved, Tex, but she regrets it now.

TEX. Fear.

SUSAN (*tense, angry*). You'll have to learn to be a bit more detached, Tracky. I know it's hard, that's what *I* have to do. When I go into the room my Mammy doesn't even look at me. So I just don't-look-at-her back.

TRACKY. It's nothing to do with my Mammy.

SUSAN. It's her that's scrambled your Daddy's brains! – I don't know why you hate your Da so much. She's the loony. So can we please solve this rationally?

TEX. Can we please put things back –

SUSAN. *Or Tex will throw an eppy.*

TEX. – together. – Put it this way, Tracky: (if I can't appeal to your emotions): I've got a *piece* of that taxi.

TRACKY. Keep it then.

TRACKY exits. Fast.

TEX. *Tracky! Will you* – ? That's frightening, that. That's –. See? Where's the fear?!

SUSAN. It's her feelings: she's getting messages but she's lost the de-coder.

TEX. Am I supposed to – feelings! – I'm supposed to do my mechanic? I've an appointment to keep!

No option but to lift the wheels back onto the pram.

SUSAN. It's OK. Everything will turn out good in the end.

TEX. Wheels! Wheels!

SUSAN. We'll get them back.

TEX. This family's: five to seven: *taking me apart.* – Right. Right. But this is going on the bill.

SUSAN. We could hide the wheels under the pram, turn the pram over and come back for them later.

TEX. Right. Right. We'll turn the pram over and . . . (what you said) right? You're OK you. I could do things with you. I thought I could get somewhere with Tracky but fuck'r she's too tense.

SUSAN (*as TEX exits pushing the pram*). Meet you over there by your car.

TEX. Right. Right.

TEX exits. SUSAN watches. And – as the scene shifts around her – she metaphorically hugs herself for joy.

Scene Three

City centre. A cash-machine. And round it or near it, police incident-ribbon, marking out a space. The ribbon is dirty, two or three days old. It's now marking out the ghost of an incident.
SAMMY *and* LUCY *come on.*

SAMMY. This is us. Cash-machine. Cash-machine. This is us.

LUCY. I still can't believe they killed it, you know. Idiots! It was a perfectly good story.

SAMMY. Cash-machine. That's us fine now. No offence.

LUCY. Of course EMI denied the rumour (what did they expect?) that's a story in itself. 'EMI DENIES RUMOURED MOVE'.

SAMMY. (You still here?) Where's Agnes? Where's Tex? Cohere, *there's* a word for you. This isn't converging.

LUCY. I don't know where I get the energy to go on sometimes.

AGNES *comes on . . . drunker than before. Her physical control is erratic, coming and going.*

AGNES. So right, I've been. Happy? 'Hurry up, Agnes,' he says. 'Hurry up'? Am I not allowed to perform my toilet now? There: put the handcuffs on: because I won't be handcuffed, not by anybody. (I see the cash-machine.)

She gets the cashcard out of her purse. As she approaches the cash-machine, she stops, turns back towards LUCY.

Ahhhch, shhhh, sorry, Lucy, sorry . . . sorry . . . sorry. Sorry. Right? Sorry.

She approaches the cash-machine again, then stops again. Then she points at the police incident-ribbon. And suddenly AGNES *is a storm.*

Oh god oh god – am I the only one that can see it? (*Oh* my breath *oh* my breath) oh I can't stay here, on a lovely summer's evening like this? (*oh* my breath) on a lovely summer's evening like this – I could drop down dead!

SAMMY. Agnes. Cash-machine.

AGNES. (drop down dead) then where would I be? (*oh* my breath *oh* my breath)

SAMMY. I could comprehend it if – but she *offered*

AGNES. no further forward, put it that way

SAMMY. only for her offering I'd've had my kicking over and
done with hours ago: I'd've recovered the feeling in my face by
now

AGNES. what do they have to do before you see it, write it in
blood? (oh my breath oh my breath)

SAMMY. I can't grasp – can you grasp – ?

AGNES. and you're walking right into it (nose against the toilet
window) as usual, *they've even mapped out where it's going to happen*

SAMMY. Give me a doing, Tex, will you. Kick my brains in.
Because I can't battle with the supernatural as well as –

TRACKY *appears.*

TRACKY. What's happening?

SAMMY. – every other thing! Your mother's turned to the dark
side: (maybe you can reach her).

LUCY. What if you gave *me* the cashcard? I could withdraw
money for you.

AGNES. Get away! (We have to get away!)

And suddenly LUCY *has very quietly and efficiently grappled with*
AGNES *and clamped her.*

LUCY. You're very frightened aren't you (in your own way). I
tell you what I do when I'm frightened, I get very very calm
and very efficient. That's the best thing to do. There: better
now? – It must be the heat. That's when my mother used to go
mad. She'd run out naked into the garden and hide behind the
rose-bushes saying she was the Virgin Queen. – Where's your
card, in your purse?

LUCY *opens her purse and takes the cashcard.*

Now what's your number?

AGNES. Oh Lucy . . . sorry . . . I'm sorry . . . sorry. I'm – . It's the
– ahch! It's the anonymity that gets me. I could be anyone.
And people! Do you never wonder. I'll tell you about
numbers . . . we're overcrowded, put it that way. Trillions of us.
And see when the world ends, then: the people that were never

born? Souls I'm talking about, souls. How can God do that, infinite, and only create so many, and clocks?: don't talk to me about clocks: *tick tick tick:* 'tick'?: is that all they can say? – Nine.

LUCY. Nine? That's the first number. Nine what?

AGNES. Nine – nine –

SAMMY. Is that two nines or the same nine?

AGNES. Nine, I'm saying. 999! This is the soul I'm talking about. Pain.

LUCY. I can't help you if you won't calm down.

TRACKY's *looking off.*

TRACKY. Look. Here comes Tex: wanting his money.

SAMMY. Don't you – where?

TRACKY. There. Sauntering down the road at a fast run.

AGNES. (*oh* my breath *oh* my breath)

SAMMY. Agnes.

AGNES. I *warned* you! Quick.

SAMMY. 'Quick'?! Quick *you!*

AGNES. Face like a blood orange (oh Sammy!). Is that a polisman? Help me, help me! Officer! Officer!

And AGNES *exits fast.*

SAMMY. Agnes! What are you – ? What's she – ? *That's a traffic warden!* Is there an explanation for that? What *is* that? Vision? Or some kind of. Some people think that's interesting, how people *get* like that – oh there we go, now she's engaged the traffic warden in fisticuffs –

TRACKY. You'd better run.

SAMMY. Because interesting, I'll tell you what's interesting: what's interesting about that? (A conversation would be interesting.)

TRACKY. Because he won't stop to talk: running jump at you.

SAMMY. Talking rubbish, that would be interesting (like we used to) . . . recipes, talk . . .

TRACKY. Run.

SAMMY. Fuck.

TRACKY. Run.

SAMMY. Fuck.

SAMMY *exits at a run. Then* TEX *enters at a run, followed by* SUSAN.

SUSAN. Should I, what will I do?

TEX. Right you. Cash. Gelt. Because it's over. Right? Over.

TRACKY. I haven't got it, Tex.

SUSAN. Look at Mrs Doak: she wannered that parky in the jaw.

TEX. Who has then? Her? Him?

SUSAN. Oh god. Blood's excellent!

TEX *produces a knife and waves it at* TRACKY *and* LUCY.

TEX. See that! See bloody that?

SUSAN. What one are *you* going to capture, Tex. Mr or Mrs?

TEX. What? (My professionalism's fucked with this family . . .) The pledge. I have to secure the pledge.

SUSAN. You won't get *Mrs Doak* off the drink.

TEX. He's the pledge – el gobshite. He's pledged his arse. Because the time's long since gone, Tracky. Those days are past.

SUSAN. I'll get Mrs Doak then.

And SUSAN *and* TEX *exit in the same direction as* AGNES *and* SAMMY *respectively.*

LUCY. I could tell you where my mother got the right pills for her, if that's any help. There's a brilliant specialist in –

TRACKY. Just give us the cashcard and don't say nothing, creep.

TRACKY *rips the cashcard off her and goes. Alone,* LUCY *gets out her phone. Makes a call.*

LUCY. Yes, hello: accounts please. – Lucy Bolt here, freelance, phoning about payment for a piece of mine you used. Yes. Could you send it onto Angela Boyd, care of, 29 Partickhill Road, Glasgow. Thanks.

Then she makes another call.

Angela. Yes – Lucy! At last: I've been ringing, oh engaged engaged engaged . . . you were out? *really*! Listen, I'm in the middle of chaos – yes, Glasgow – my hotel double-booked me and I'm due to interview (oh, *you* know, *nobody*) in, five minutes ago, I can't believe this is happening to me – could I crash at your place tonight? . . . yes *everywhere*, well everywhere I can afford, there's some big conference going on or something . . . oh Angela, thanks . . . thanks . . . thanks . . . thanks . . . thanks . . . yes, about ten, nine, earlier if I can cut it short . . . thanks . . . thanks . . . bye.

She puts the phone away. Recovers herself from the difficulty of the phone call and exits.
TEX *enters and takes a running jump at the cash-machine.*

TEX. Missed him. Missed him. *Missed* him. Thin air.

As TEX *takes a final kick or punch at the uncomprehending banking facility,* SUSAN *enters with Mrs Doak's bag.*

SUSAN. Tex. Look what I got: Mrs Doak's bag. Don't worry, she dropped it.

And she empties the contents of the bag onto the ground, looking for the cashcard.

Look at this. Rubbish. Rubbish. Polo mints. More rubbish. Chinky ribs.

TEX. Mess! I've got a lovely semi-detached in Newlands! Red sandstone. Solid. Like: solid. Big garden for wee Christopher to run amok in.

SUSAN. No cashcard.

TEX. I could be sitting on the steps watching him. *'Stead of having my insides spilled out on the pavement.*

He's pointing at the contents of Mrs Doak's bag, as if it's his insides. Then –

Pension books. Invalidity books. Giros. Or they dig you out a letter from their doctor, the prescriptions they're on.
Bronchitis. Angina. Their heart. Skin. Lungs. Knees. Hips. And then they want to be pleasant to you. 'You're just like my big son', they say. Then they tell you about their big son.

Pause. SUSAN *wants to say something that might take his mind off what he is.*

SUSAN. Listen, Tex. I know it's shite you being in a band, right, but I really believe it, even though I know it's shite. And you were dead honest about it, you never even said you were, I just made it up. Because. So. So what, right?

Pause.

TEX. You're OK you. After this (seeing as how *you're* being honest with *me*) there's a flat over Ibrox way. Council house: high rise. My Granny died so I kept it on . . . so I could escape away, listen to my albums. You could practically move in.

SUSAN. Oh god. I think so! I don't want to do anything too fast.

TEX. I *say* 'move in'. Put it this way: it's there. Whenever.

SAMMY *returns: to take what's coming to him.*

SAMMY. Tex. I came back.

TEX. You? – Go away.

SAMMY *obeys.*

Come here. Answer me this: why did I tell you to go away? Go away, I said. Here's another question. Cash? No? Cashcard? No? – So right. So you're here. Now what? So you're an out-and-out never-to-be-repeated *pranny:* I'm enriched. Thank you. Thank you for that. And that's what you're offering me (and me that wades through pensioners in my sleep) and I have to *do* something with that. I have to respond. Well fuck off. You've come here and offered me an insight (which is something I knew already) and now the onus is on *me?* – I'm 21. You see my point.

SAMMY. (Doing) doing fair enough, I'll *take* that. But you'd lost the place back there: I think you'd acknowledge that. You'd have ran right through me.

TEX *may be on the verge of killing him, when –*

SUSAN. Tex. Here's Mrs Doak coming.

TEX *goes for* SAMMY *and collars him. Knuckles him on the head, hard.*

TEX. One-last-chance. One-last-chance.

AGNES *enters. By now she's ripped her tights, skinned her knees, lost her bag, and cut her face in the fight with the traffic warden . . . she is a desolate, lost and flailing soul.*

AGNES. (grab grab grab) Glasgow? Glasgow? Ask a traffic
warden a simple question. 'Glasgow' – *I'm* Glasgow. And I'm
left with nothing. Coat? you want my coat, Sammy? Because
take it, what do I need with a coat, I'm only –. Can you
understand that? Because *you* tell *me*. Of course I'm only – I
work for the biggest employer in the country! I'm in pain! I'm
in jail!

*And she beats her knuckled fists against the bars of her prison: her
forehead. Then, as this outburst subsides –*

I can't even. Oh Sammy. Help me. I don't ask you often do I.
Just when I'm alone and I can't take any more.

The pathos of a drunken desperate plea. SAMMY *is moved despite
himself. Crosses to her and holds her.*

SAMMY (*weary tenderness*). I'm here, Agnes. I'm here, pet. What
have you done to yourself, eh gorgeous?

AGNES. Oh Sammy.

SAMMY. Come on and sit down.

AGNES. I just wanted to help you, Sammy.

SAMMY. I know you did. Hope? What hope's there for me when
I'm still in *love* with you, eh?

AGNES. . . . after all the lies I've told you . . .

SAMMY. Still in love with you.

AGNES. And (the mess I've made, the state I'm in) . . .

SAMMY. Ahch. We all deserve (better than we get), don't we?

SUSAN. It's OK, Mrs Doak. We found your bag.

AGNES. Bag?

SUSAN. Look.

SUSAN *picks up the bottle of alcohol off the pavement and brings it
over to* AGNES.

AGNES' (*eyes following the bottle*). Oh my *bag*.

SUSAN. And look: here's another thing. Ta-rah!

She shows AGNES *her 'engagement ring'.*

I'm engaged. It's still unofficial and we're not really telling
people yet but I'm so happy I can't wait.

AGNES *admires the ring, which* SUSAN *has thrust in front of her nose.*

AGNES. Oh look: it's (what's that, Susan?) is it a skull?

SUSAN. It's a deathshead! Don't ask me who the chap is, I can't tell you. He's married.

TEX. I'm saying nothing.

SUSAN. So we have to be careful meantime. Where's your cashcard, Mrs Doak. Because Tex is getting understandably crazed and it's not in your handbag so don't say that.

And as she speaks, she starts to go through AGNES' *pockets, with complete lack of ceremony or embarrassment.*

AGNES. Am I stupid or something? What did I tell you: the ones that mugged me have got it! And get your hands out my pockets!

SUSAN. I'm only trying to help you!

AGNES. And (what?) do an internal while you're there, while you're about it, put my legs up in stirrups *because explore away.* (What am I?) And – bag? – to hell with my bag. *My kidney donor card* was in that bag but they don't think of that, do they?

SUSAN. OK: fine: solve your own problems then: because I'm trying to help *everyone.* But give up Susan, I can't co-exist at this level.

AGNES. I'd give it to you if I had it, Sammy: you know that.

TEX. So the cashcard's vanished?

SUSAN. Does the SS still give people Mobility Allowance? It probably does, Mr Doak. Because you might be *better off* in a wheelchair, once you do your sums . . .

SAMMY *indicates the handbag and contents.*

SAMMY. Tex . . . want me to take one last look?

He goes over, looking amongst the contents, using his feet.

I know it's not there, right enough. But might be might be. Because hope springs. And Glasgow, you know yourself, Tex . . . Glasgow . . .

TRACKY *enters.*

TRACKY. If you're looking for her cashcard I've got it. And I know the number as well, she sends me for her carry-outs.

SAMMY. Momentous, Tracky, momentous! (What was I just saying?) So forget my harsh words regards my wheels, Tracky (which I forgot to say, by the way) because forgive and forget, that's my approach.

TRACKY. But I can't give you it 'less you promise to sell the taxi.

SAMMY. Kids? Ahch, they're only kids, aren't they?

TRACKY. You're fixated on that taxi. And *Glasgow* (makes my stomach turn to mud) *Glasgow:* where's that? You'll be dead soon! I mean: car smash?: let's get totalled – So can we please sort our finances.

SUSAN. That's all Tex wants too.

TRACKY. Because I've snapped.

SAMMY. Taxi? Know what I call my taxi? Agnes. Because it's not the taxi that's the problem. Take away the costs, that taxi makes me a hundred, hundred and fifty a week. So finances: look elsewhere.

TRACKY. We're in debt, Da!

SAMMY. Can I say one thing and leave it at that? And another thing: who buys the food! The only thing I asked her to pay for was the telly. Then when the telly people came to re-possess it, she flung the stereo at them. (That's how much economics she knows.) So just give me the card.

SUSAN. Don't get all emotional, Tracky.

SAMMY. *Get* emotional! This is your Daddy here. This is your Daddy with a sore face in a minute.

SUSAN. Don't, Mr Doak: you don't know what you're talking about: she hates you.

SAMMY (*shocked*). (Hates me?)

TRACKY. Susan, you are so true blue. Loyal?

SAMMY. (My daughter?) What way hates me? Actually hates me? So OK, I'll acknowledge I've been over-preoccupied the last few weeks . . . but that's just the usual. What about the time – ? I mean, what about Kenny? Agnes, were you aware of this?

AGNES. Oh don't involve me. Father and daughter?

SAMMY. She's only young all the same. Kids: they're just kids aren't they: no wonder the pygmies *eat* theirs. Obscure? Will I tell you why you hate *me?* Because if you hated her she wouldn't even notice! (I've tried it.)

AGNES. Blame me suddenly.

TRACKY. She only drinks because of you.

AGNES. Drink: where's the sentence (sense): a minute ago it was finances.

TRACKY. Look at the states of her: hanging onto her brains. And you stand there. I'm *eight* and I'm waiting on you to *do* something. And now I'm fifteen I'm *still* waiting.

SAMMY. Tracky, you're all confused, darlin'.

TRACKY. And all I get: tears: begging her: what use are tears? And Glasgow? Glasgow? Can you *explain* that to me?

AGNES. (He knows nothing about Glasgow: I'm Glasgow.)

TRACKY. And on and on and on (I don't even want to discuss it) it just goes on and on and on.

SAMMY. And what do you want me to do, *take her wheels off?*

AGNES. Ahch . . . (what's it matter).

SAMMY. *Take her wheels off?*

TRACKY *is stopped in her tracks. For a moment anyway.*

TRACKY. And then there was the time we're flying back from Malta

SAMMY. (where are we now?)

TRACKY. I'm eight and we're flying back from Malta

SAMMY. time (back and forwards like Einstein) I can't keep up

TRACKY. back from Malta and she slaps me in the face for nothing, because I was excited or something

SAMMY. where's this again?

TRACKY. (oh don't deny it) she slaps me in the face and about (so many minutes later) you and her are snogging . . . you and her are snogging . . . you and her are snogging . . .

TRACKY *wipes at her eyes with her arm.*

You never even told her off. She slaps me. So I sit there nearly greetin and nobody says nothing for like ten minutes. Then you and her start talking, then – five minutes – you turn your back on me and – start.

Upset for TRACKY, SAMMY *is reduced to tentative self-justifications.*

SAMMY. (Sudden urges she gets). (Was I trying to placate her?) – So she slaps you in the face, *I'm* to blame?

TRACKY. so right: so I'm to blame?

SAMMY. blame me because your logic's (circuitry's – jinxed)

TRACKY. blame me because I got sent to the psychiatrist's or something

SAMMY. blame me then

TRACKY. because I'm maladjusted and don't know when I'm supposed to be happy or what different feelings I should be feeling *when* and so nobody likes me

SAMMY. blame me because I marry this lovely person and we're walking hand in hand and suddenly turn round and I'm holding a snake she's turned into a snake and I don't know where she's gone to!

AGNES. Ho: I baffled the lot of them. Psychiatrists? I out-thought them. This one says to me: you're obviously deeply unhappy, Mrs Doak. So I'm too smart for him, I just nod profoundly. Ha- haaaah! I just nod profoundly. Brains. – (Ahch, shhh) . . . *nobody* understands my pain. Nobody. *My pain is my pain* . . . and (that's it). – That's how I'm so alone. Because I've too much brains for you.

She batters some more drink down her throat. SAMMY *and* TRACKY *watch her, baffled, lost. Then* TRACKY *throws down the cashcard. A gesture of hopelessness. And because she sees, however obscurely, that the cashcard isn't the point.*

TRACKY. What's it matter? We're all going to die anyway, right? – 9367.

SAMMY. If you're –

TRACKY. Try it.

SAMMY goes to the machine, inserts the card etc. AGNES, *after the last injection of whisky, is now only just hanging onto her brains.*

AGNES. . . . alone? Oh don't kid yourself . . . alone? Ahch, shhh
. . . I'm saying nothing.

SAMMY. I'm in.

AGNES. . . . speech? Oh soley . . . will I tell you because? Because
because.

SAMMY. What service do I require? – sorry, sorry, sorry Tex,
pressed the wrong thing – statement . . .

AGNES. . . . ffff – whaws: ling: am ah?: ahch! (shut up, Agnes)

SAMMY. . . . here it's coming, Tex: haw: listen to . . .

SAMMY *gets statement out of machine and reads it – as background
to –*

TEX. Cash-machines, eh? There was a time when, if you'd no
money that was you –

SAMMY. Ten quid.

TEX. – skinto.

SAMMY. That's her lot. Ten quid. She took out eighty earlier on
today. – Checked her purse?

TEX. Checked it. Smash. Coins.

SAMMY. Checked her purse? What? You've checked it. Checked it.

AGNES. . . . because I still wake up sweating, don't I? . . . money
. . . is that the only reason (swarming round me) . . . ahch
money . . . ahch shhhh I'm sorry . . . I'm sorry . . . I'm sorry . . .
I'm sorry Sammy . . .
burns?

With one final effort she lifts her head and explains what happened.

. . . Margaret at my work . . . she was *at* me for her fifty . . .
bank was *at* me . . . monkeys jumping on my back and hanging
onto (my hair), will you get – ? So I paid them, didn't I? Paid
them. Then you . . . then I come and see you . . . welcome? . . .
then you wanted . . . then you ask(ed) . . .

SAMMY. You offered, Agnes.

AGNES. Naw, you *never* asked, you *never* asked, I was too low-
class or something! . . . I just wanted . . . to help you, Sammy
. . . I just wanted to

help. Ahch, shhhhh . . . work tomorrow . . .

And her head falls forward. SAMMY lifts her head to look at her. She's asleep.

SAMMY. She's asleep.

TEX. Samuel, Samuel. (So that the prophecy might be fulfilled.) So that's the onus on me. – Take your time: wait for me up that lane.

SAMMY goes. TEX looks at them, keeping SAMMY waiting. He gives SUSAN his jacket and walks up the lane. There's a series of sickening groans as SAMMY gets done over, and after six or seven serious blows there's the sound of retching. Just as we think this signals the doing is over, there are three more vicious knocks and semi-conscious exhalations of pain. Then TEX says, 'Next Saturday, Sammy son. Cash.'
TEX enters, wipes spats of blood from his face and takes his jacket from SUSAN who can't look at him properly. TEX looks at them as if to say 'What's your problem?' Goes.
Silence. Then SUSAN goes to look up the lane.

TRACKY. Is he moving?

SUSAN. Not yet.

Helpless pause.

TRACKY. At least something's *happened*. Something's a bit more clearer now. – Will I phone an ambulance?

SUSAN. Phone an ambulance and the police will come.

TRACKY. Well don't blame me, Susan: I was only trying to (warn him.)

SUSAN. It's OK. He's moving. He's getting up.

TRACKY. What's he like?

SUSAN. Oh god.

TRACKY. Don't look then.

SUSAN. Phone an ambulance.

TRACKY. You're enjoying this!

SUSAN. He's coming!

SAMMY comes on. As it happens, he walks through into the space

marked out by the incident-ribbon, like he's the accident that's been
waiting to happen. He's a mess. Can't walk right. Speaks like his face
is swollen. TRACKY *finds it hard to look at him. He finds it hard to*
look at her.

TRACKY. (oh Daddy.)

SAMMY. One piece.

SUSAN (*upset*). It had to happen, Mr Doak! (*Then she tries to*
retrieve that sentence.) (I'm sorry) it had to happen.

SAMMY *looks at* AGNES. *Asleep.*

SAMMY. And look at her. My flesh and blood. – I better go to
the hospital. Or my brother's. Maybe I can stay there
temporary till I get (fixed up). How d'you fancy staying at your
Uncle Jim's Aunt Margaret's? Your mother . . . I can't live with
her, Tracky. It's too . . . *sore*.

TRACKY. Leave us?

SAMMY. I beg her. I plead with her. Is it *me* that's at fault: *I*
have to go then. Because I'm baffled.

TRACKY. She wanted to help you.

SAMMY. I know she did.

TRACKY. It wasn't badness. She wanted to help you so she just
said she had money.

SAMMY. I know, pet.

TRACKY. Because she *felt* bad she'd no *money*. Uncle Jim's? –
That's like you: run away: easy: never turn and face facts.
What about her?

SAMMY. Look at her, Tracky. And look at me. Who pays the
bills? Who's stupid? And every time she goes out or she's late
back my stomach's going that something's happened to her, a
road-accident. Or she's met some bloke. And while I'm busy
worrying about *her:* this! – And Glasgow: and my taxi: OK so I
kid myself on. So it's a lovely summer's evening, why not? *Why*
not kid myself on it's a lovely summer's evening? – Because I love
her so bad, but I can't raise her from the dead.

Pause.

TRACKY. Go then.

SAMMY. Tracky.

SUSAN. Leave her here?

SAMMY. So you get her home, then what?

TRACKY. Put her to bed. Look after her.

SAMMY. Like a baby? And (baby?) – how is she? – put a four month-old baby on the carpet, and it starts doing exercises: arms, legs, roll-overs. I don't know what I'm talking about here . . . (hope). What I'm trying to express is (can you not *see?*) your mother stops drinking when she falls unconscious.

TRACKY. That's *your* attitude.

SAMMY. And you think you can stop her? You're *better* than me?

TRACKY *refuses to answer this.*

TRACKY. On you go then, go. You were useless to me anyway.

SAMMY *considers his options one last time. He decides to go. But before he does –*

SAMMY. See being unhappy, Tracky: don't get too fond of it.

And he goes.
Pause. Then TRACKY *crosses to look after him. A fifteen year-old girl who wants her Daddy, wants her Daddy more than anything.*

SUSAN. Aw, cheer up. We're all going to die anyway, what's it matter? How about we get crazed up on some smarties 'n' lager and hit the dance-floor.

TRACKY. Then what?

SUSAN. Then we get utterly blind, pass out and wake up somewhere utterly crazy like Oban. I could *do* with getting my hole.

TRACKY. Ya slack cow! What about . . . chick.

SUSAN. Fuck chick. Coming? Your Ma's got a coupla pound coins in her purse.

TRACKY. And what'll we do with her?

SUSAN. Take her with us! Leave her here! We'll get her on the way back.

TRACKY. Give us that purse over here.

SUSAN. See now I'm not involved, I feel like really free. Check me on the dance-floor, I'll be like that – shaking my hair at them. Where'll we go first, The Bowff?

TRACKY. I'm sick of The Bowff, we've been going there since we were twelve. Plus the fact this is my housekeeping. This is all I've got to do me the week.

SUSAN. Aw Tracky . . .

TRACKY. Aw grow up, Susan! Sex is for kids. – Help me get her shifted.

SUSAN. She's paralytic.

TRACKY. Just help us, will you?

They struggle with AGNES' *dead weight. A hopeless task.*

SUSAN. Where are we going with her? Because a taxi won't take her.

TRACKY. You're not lifting her.

SUSAN. I am.

TRACKY. Well don't be so delicate.

They resume the struggle.

Aw come on, Mammy.

In exasperation she gives her mother a wee kick.

Will you –

She gives her another wee kick. Then she kicks her hard.

I'm trying to help you, Mammy!

THE BABY

The Baby was first staged at the Tron Theatre, Glasgow on 13 October, 1990 with the following cast:

GOBBER	Peter Grimes
RUFUS	Ross Dunsmore
FLOOD	Anne Lacey
MACU	Rosaleen Pelan
EMILIA	Jennifer Black
WOCKY	Billy McColl
CRASSUS	John Stahl
MARCELLA	Hilary Maclean
RANA	Jenny McCrindle
POMPEY	Ross Dunsmore
SORCHA	John Stahl
LAURA	Jenny McCrindle
USHLA	Jenny McCrindle
RANEE, a healer	Anne Lacey
SIZE	John Stahl
OFFICER	Ross Dunsmore
GRIN	Peter Grimes
BUTTER	Ross Dunsmore
OOLA	Jenny McCrindle
JALATA	Jennifer Black
AYEESHA	Hilary Maclean
ZUZIBARRA	Anne Lacey
NUDDY	Jennifer Black
PHYLLIDA	Hilary Maclean
JOPPA	Peter Grimes
SHARMA	Jenny McCrindle
1ST TORMENTOR	Jennifer Black
2ND TORMENTOR	Peter Grimes
3RD TORMENTOR	Jenny McCrindle
VOCALISTS	Jennifer Black
	Hilary Maclean

Directed by Michael Boyd
Designed by Rae Smith
Lighting by Nick McCall
Music composed by Craig Armstrong

ACT ONE

Scene One

Broad daylight. Two RIOTERS *come on running, spattered in blood.*

RIOTER 1. Scatter!

RIOTER 2. We kicked his head off.

RIOTER 1. Move!

RIOTER 2. I'm kicking away, all of a sudden his head's like a slack tooth. We kicked his head off!

RIOTER 1. I was holding them back. They climbed over me!

RIOTER 2. We were all kicking at him, you too.

RIOTER 1. Wipe the blood off your neck. You've got blood on your neck.

RIOTER 2. So! The whole mob's out. Kicking down shops and throwing pails of cowblood at anyone stands in their way. I won't look different from anyone else.

RIOTER 1. Come on then. Let's get out of here.

They go.

Scene Two

Daylight. A street. MACU *comes on, trying on a sarong. She sees* EMILIA.

MACU. Emilia! Emilia!

Having caught EMILIA's *attention, she mouths the next bit silently.*

Come and see what I found.

EMILIA *enters.* MACU *shows off her new sarong.*

MACU. Do you like it? They're lying all over the street down there. Silk.

EMILIA. Silk?

MACU. Here, you have it. I don't think it's my colour. – What are they doing over there?

EMILIA. They're gutting a flower-stall.

MACU. Oh look – there's Laura!

MACU *waves at* LAURA.

She doesn't see me.

EMILIA. Would she not be safer at home? She's only eight, Macu.

MACU *calls* LAURA.

MACU. Laura! Laura!

LAURA *comes in, carrying a battered wreath. The flowers in the wreath are white, the colour of mourning and death.*

LAURA. Look what I got, mammy, do you think I can sell it?

MACU. A wreath?

LAURA. Then I could buy something proper. Sweets or something.

MACU. Should you not be at home? You'll get hurt.

LAURA. I'm with Wocky and Yanis! You should see what they're doing to the stalls. It's like watching an accident, only better.

MACU. Well stay next to Emilia then. I'm going to get myself some clothes.

MACU *goes.* LAURA *is more interested in what's happening in the other direction.*

LAURA. Look! They're chasing him over here.

EMILIA. Come here out of the way, Laura.

WOCKY, YANIS *and one or two others come on with poles and sticks etc, which they're using to bait and threaten a* FLOWER-SELLER. *They're enjoying themselves.*

FLOWER-SELLER. Please, I'm new here. What do I know? I only get off the boat yesterday. My brother, this is my brother's stall. He ask me to sell the flowers.

WOCKY. I don't see any flowers, do you, Yanis?

YANIS. All I see are wreaths.

WOCKY. A whole stall and nothing but wreaths. Does he always sell nothing but wreaths, your brother?

WOCKY *holds up a wreath on his pole while* YANIS *smashes it with a stick.*

FLOWER-SELLER. You stupid fucks. You are the worst of men. You throw unclean blood over my shop, you've polluted the streets, by the way. You have no respect even for your own gods and this why you turn everything upside down. Yahweh protect me from you, God protect me. Sulla dies – who is this man? – he's the greatest man in all Rome – yes, the greatest man. Do you cry, do you stay inside and say prayers? No, you turn the streets into like – shipwrecks – and you say this man Sulla, this your – king, this man will not even have a funeral. Yaaah – and women do this, and little girls, by the way. You are nothing but dirty fanny. Yes I sell wreaths – Sulla dies and many people buy wreaths for him, today and tomorrow they buy for Sulla's funeral. Good boy, Sulla!

YANIS. Dirty Arab. Kick his head off.

LAURA. Kick his dirty head off. What does he know?

WOCKY. There's Macu. – Macu! Macu! Come here and listen to this. This one talks. – She's coming. This is the woman I was telling you about, Yanis, the one with the temper. Watch this, she'll tear his head off.

MACU *comes on, trying on another new sarong.*

Macu. This one here was selling wreaths.

MACU. So he's a stupid bastard, what do you want *me* to do? – Come here a minute, Wocky.

WOCKY *goes over.*

Do you think this colour sarong goes with my hair, I know it doesn't but say I got it dyed.

WOCKY. Got it dyed what?

MACU. I don't know yet, it depends what jewellery I can get. – Leave him be.

WOCKY. On you go, Yahweh. We're busy.

As the FLOWER-SELLER *passes* MACU, *he spits at her.*

FLOWER-SELLER. Dirty fanny!

WOCKY *jumps at him.*

YANIS. Shut his mouth!

FLOWER-SELLER. Dirty cunt!

MACU. Why does he think that? Did you show him your prick, Wocky?

EMILIA. Laura! Come here to me.

MACU. Laura! You should be home.

FLOWER-SELLER. You should all be home. You think you can stop this man's funeral? You're only some, you think you're a lot but you're only some, I know how many wreaths I sell. Sulla was a great man. I come here with my cousins, nine years ago we have nothing. Now we have three stalls.

WOCKY. Two stalls.

FLOWER-SELLER. Listen to me! Listen to me! You wreck my shop, you listen to me for a change. I remember how it was before there was Sulla. Too much taxes, too much doles. Men hire out mobs to cause troubles because they want to make money and other men want to make troubles. One day I'm walking home and I slip on my arse. It's someone's brains I slip on! I have a stall then too. One day I open, tomorrow I'm bankrupt. Then Sulla makes peace. Cut taxes. Good boy, Sulla, no way. No more troublemakers. What's wrong you don't like this man?

WOCKY. Ho! Tell him, Macu.

MACU. I've got an eight year old girl can tell you why. – On you go, Laura. Tell Yabba why we hate Sulla. Don't be frightened, tell him.

Silence. So MACU *prompts.*

MACU. (He took away the vote.)

LAURA. He took away the vote!

MACU. And what else did he do? (He took away the doles.)

LAURA. He took away the doles!

MACU. Good girl.

LAURA. He took away the vote and he took away the doles!

This goes down well, so she tries it again.

He took away the vote and he took away the doles! He took away the vote and he took away the doles!

She's run out of script now, but she wants to go on and crown her success.

Then Sulla said the people weren't allowed any more, then everyone was angry but I wasn't allowed to say anything because my daddy didn't like it, then my daddy ran away with a Greek bitch.

Silence. Maybe stifled laughter from YANIS.

EMILIA. Come here to me, Laura.

When MACU *next speaks, it's to the* FLOWER-SELLER. *We are uncertain at first whether she's talking about* SULLA *or her husband. So is she.*

MACU. Ho! The man turned my stomach. He was putrid. He'd jump on anything, he was in and out of everything, man, woman or beast. Me? I don't even know who I was then, I felt like I was wearing someone else's skin. Do you know what I do for a living? I cry. I'm a mourner. I put on my dead clothes and I walk behind a funeral hearse and I howl. I tear the sky open. Have I got to do that for Sulla? The man tore my throat out. He was putrid.

She stops. There's a moment. Then she picks up a wreath and starts hitting the FLOWER-SELLER *with it.*
FLOOD *comes on.*

FLOOD. Come on, we're all going to Crassus's.

EMILIA. Flood.

FLOOD. Come on, Macu.

WOCKY. What's happening?

FLOOD. All the mourners are going to see Crassus. Come on, Wocky. Come on, Emilia.

FLOOD *goes.*

WOCKY. Come on or we'll miss it. Leave Yahweh his wreaths. He can watch them rot.

MACU. You'd better pray there's a plague.

EMILIA. You go, Macu. I'll take Laura home.

LAURA. I don't want to go home.

MACU. You go with Emilia and I'll bring you something back.

WOCKY. Come on. Let's go then.

> MACU *goes with* WOCKY *and* YANIS, LAURA *with* EMILIA. *The* FLOWER-SELLER *is left with his battered wreaths. He picks them up and goes.*

Scene Three

CRASSUS *appears on a balcony, putting on a stole the colour of mourning. Off, there's the sound of the mourners making an unholy noise. They use maracas, Tibetan-type bells, voice and whatever else. As mourners, they are well-equipped to inspire onlookers with supernatural dread.*
Then they come on. MACU, WOCKY, FLOOD, YANIS, *plus others.*

FLOOD. It's us, Crassus.

YANIS. Are you in mourning for someone?

FLOOD. Have you not heard, Crassus? A senator who was wearing mourning got his two hands cut off.

WOCKY. The things he'll never feel again.

MACU. Arse!

YANIS. Stone. I can't tell you how good it feels to hold a stone in your hand.

CRASSUS. I put on mourning when I heard you were coming: I thought it would cheer you up. Someone's dead: you should be celebrating. Sulla's dead! – I was there at his deathbed, my friends. And I can tell you, death has never wanted anyone as much as it wanted Sulla. History will say, he was the first man ever to be eaten by worms *before* he died. His whole body was heaving with them, there was more of worms than there was of him, yet even to the end he was all appetite, feeding figs through a hole in his face while the worms crawled out of his eyes. Out of his eyes, my friends! And then it was over.

Silence.

You know me: I'm not a superstitious man. But I went to the Temple afterwards and offered a sacrifice. I wanted to get the smell of him out of my hair.

FLOOD. And this is what they want to give a state funeral.

MACU. Take him out and dig him into the compost.

FLOOD. Tell the senate, Crassus: there's not a mourner in Rome will mourn for Sulla. We'll walk behind that rotting corpse in silence.

YANIS. The gods won't even know he's dead.

CRASSUS. And what good will that do you? Eh? Where will that get you? – Sulla's dead. Nobody's asking you to be sad about it. Nobody's asking you to take a collection. You're mourners. That's your job. You cry when you're paid to cry. So – you howl for Sulla, then go off and forget the bastard ever existed. Am I talking sense or what? The priest sets fire to that funeral pyre and Sulla's just another kebab.

MACU. Sense or nonsense, what's the difference?

FLOOD. We're not doing it, Crassus. It's as simple as that.

MACU. Better they bury Sulla in a back garden somewhere. Like a dead cat.

CRASSUS. Use your brains, my friends. There's going to be a funeral, whether you like it or not. If you won't do it, we'll just have to bring in mourners from somewhere else. Naples. Brindisi.

Threatening noises, the hiss of maracas, ululations. As if we're in the presence of the dead.

FLOOD. You do that and you'll remember it, Crassus, every time you put food in your stomach. All your days you'll have a sick feeling in your stomach, you'll eat like a man before his wife's funeral. When you look at your wife, you'll think of an open grave, she'll wonder why you don't want her any more. When she lies there and opens her arms, you'll go down to her like a gravedigger into the hole, into the grave he's digging for a small child. – Joy? You'll grind your teeth in your sleep. When you look at a new born baby you'll cry.

Cymbal sounds etc. CRASSUS *is shaken.*

CRASSUS. Give me time. Let me look into it. I'll tell the senate how you feel. I'll do all I can.

CRASSUS retreats to cheers, jeers etc. The mourners disperse in triumph, leaving MACU, FLOOD, YANIS *and* WOCKY.

MACU. Wooooh!

FLOOD. Where's the drink?

WOCKY. Give the woman a drink.

YANIS. You cursed him slack.

MACU. I wish I could curse like that. I'd go hunt my husband and curse him till his balls shrank away to this size.

YANIS. Beans.

MACU. Smaller.

EMILIA. You'd better behave yourself, Wocky.

WOCKY. Me? I keep on her good side.

MACU. He might stand there and smirk but inside he'd shrink away like a man's prick in the cold.

WOCKY. That's her husband she's talking about.

A WOMAN *comes on.*

WOMAN. Flood. Lepidus has gone to the Forum to talk to the people.

MACU. Lepidus?

FLOOD. The consul? What's he got to say?

WOMAN. He's speaking out against Sulla. Are you coming?

WOCKY, FLOOD *and* YANIS *go to follow the* WOMAN.

MACU. Leave us some drink.

FLOOD. Are you not coming?

MACU. We'll catch you up.

The others go. WOCKY *takes the hint and stays.*

MACU. So!

WOCKY. So!

MACU. Some day.

WOCKY. I wish you wouldn't talk about him.

MACU. Who?

WOCKY. Your husband. You talk about him and your tongue's like an old razor. Don't *think* about him.

MACU. I don't! – So come here and give me a kiss then.

WOCKY. Here?

MACU. Yes!

WOCKY. I've got blood on my hands.

MACU. Hold my face.

They kiss. Then they look at each other.

WOCKY. You're some woman. Every time I try and grasp you, you jump out of my hands like tapwater.

She slides away from him.

WOCKY. You kept disappearing today. Every time I turned round, you'd vanished.

MACU. You didn't look for me very hard.

WOCKY. Was I supposed to?

MACU. Do you remember the warehouse?

WOCKY. The one that had linen and silks and went on for miles, and it was all underground so everything was lovely and cool, and you disappeared for about an hour and nobody knew where you'd got to? What about it?

MACU. I was lying in a big soft pile of linen. Waiting for you.

   WOCKY: *despair.*

WOCKY. Oh fuck. I thought . . . I was . . .

MACU. Come on we'll catch them up.

WOCKY. Will you come to my house tonight?

MACU. I'll have to leave Laura at Emilia's again.

She starts to go.

Come on and I'll think about it. Maybe.

She goes.

WOCKY. Maybe? Maybe? – Macu! Macu!

He goes after her.

Scene Four

POMPEY *and* MARCELLA *come on in dressing-gowns of exotic, possibly Indian, fabric and style.*

POMPEY. Rana! Rana! – What's going on out there?

MARCELLA. I don't know. I've been in bed with *you* for three days, remember?

POMPEY. Rana! Rana!

MARCELLA. Is there any food? I'm starving.

POMPEY. Rana!

RANA *comes in.*

RANA. Yes, Pompey.

POMPEY. What's going on out there, carnival? I thought I heard them shouting someone's name.

RANA. They're carrying Lepidus home to the suburbs.

POMPEY. Lepidus?

RANA. He made a speech in the Forum. He said Sulla should be scraped off his death-bed, and burnt with his bedding.

POMPEY. Lepidus? That old coffin-dodger. I thought he was confined to his bed.

RANA *clears her throat ironically.* LEPIDUS *wasn't confined to his bed,* POMPEY *was.*

RANA. How's Marcella?

MARCELLA. I've had three days of more or less continuous sex, how do you think I am? Sore. Does he love me, do you think? I can't tell.

RANA. He probably doesn't know himself.

POMPEY. Go and order me some food. Some duck or nuts or something.

RANA. Food – women – he doesn't know what he wants and he wants it now.

POMPEY. Now! Food!

RANA *goes*.

POMPEY. So it's happening then.

MARCELLA. What is?

POMPEY. Someone's made a move.

MARCELLA. Out there you're talking about.

POMPEY. While I stayed in bed.

MARCELLA. That'll end up in a tangle of limbs too. Would you rather have been out there?

POMPEY. I want power.

MARCELLA. Why did you stay in bed then?

He can't say.

POMPEY. Sex – after a day of it you don't know what bits are you and what bits are the other person. – I wanted *them* to come to *me*, that's why.

MARCELLA. The people?

POMPEY. Yes.

Slight pause as MARCELLA *takes this in*.

MARCELLA. You're so young sometimes. Well, you're young all the time, it's just sometimes I notice it. Sweet though, in a young bastard sort of way. So for three whole shagging days and nights your thoughts have been elsewhere. Have they?

POMPEY. No. – Sometimes.

MARCELLA. Oh well. Life is sweet.

RANA *comes on with food. She's followed by* SORCHA.

RANA. Pompey. There's some senators to see you. Sorcha brought them.

POMPEY. Sorcha.

SORCHA. General.

POMPEY. Senators? Who?

SORCHA. Catulus, Metellus, Crassus.

MARCELLA. They're not exactly friends of the people, what do they want?

SORCHA. Power. I would imagine. They want rid of Lepidus. They've come to you.

POMPEY. What made them think of me? I've always spoken out on the people's side.

SORCHA. You're a young, successful, popular general.

RANA. They wanted to see you privately. I took them to the garden.

POMPEY. You stay with Marcella. I'll speak to them on my own.

He goes.

RANA. Food?

SORCHA *takes some.* MARCELLA *doesn't.*

MARCELLA. Will he be safe?

SORCHA. Safe?

MARCELLA. Safe!

SORCHA. They're not going to stab him, if that's what you mean. – They'll make him an offer. So long as he turns it down, he's *safe.*

Slight pause as she takes this in.

MARCELLA. You want him to take it.

SORCHA. Don't you? I want people to love him. – How long have you known him?

MARCELLA. Long enough.

SORCHA. Has he told you about his father's funeral?

MARCELLA. No.

SORCHA. His father was the most hated man in Rome. When he died, the mob ambushed the funeral procession and threw things at the corpse. Eventually, they dragged the body from the funeral bier and tore it to bits. Pompey just watched – he was ten at the time. I went with him to the country the week after, his mother sent me. I thought he'd forgotten how to speak. One day we went fishing. I asked him what he wanted to be when he grew up. He said, 'Popular'. – I want the whole of Rome to love him.

RANA. Marcella. He's coming.

POMPEY *comes back.*

POMPEY. Rana. Make sure none of the servants leave the house. And bring some water to my room. I've got blood on my hands.

RANA *goes.*

MARCELLA. Blood.

POMPEY. We cut our hands and made a vow. Leave us for a moment, Marcella.

MARCELLA. I'll go and talk to the servants.

She goes.

POMPEY. Can you find me some dagger-men?

SORCHA. What do you want them to do?

POMPEY. Get rid of Ledipus. And clear the streets. I want Sulla to be buried in peace. – It was Sulla that made me a general. He was like a father to me. I want the people to know I'm doing this as a son.

SORCHA. The people love you, Pompey. They'll understand.

POMPEY. Thank you.

SORCHA *makes to go.*

Sorcha. I want to say this. There was a big moon out there. When I made my vow, I wanted to cry. I felt consecrated.

Pause.

SORCHA. I understand.

POMPEY. Report to me in the morning.

SORCHA *goes.* POMPEY *looks at his bloody hands.*

As if there had been something the matter with me and now everything was going to be alright again.

He gently washes his face with his hands. Then goes.

Rana! Rana!

Scene Five

Day. MACU *and* EMILIA *come on pushing a pram, which is piled up with more stuff they've looted, including wigs.*

EMILIA. Look at this one.

MACU. Waaaaaaaah! – That suits you. It makes you look like –

EMILIA. Shh!

MACU. What?

EMILIA. Has it gone quiet all of a sudden?

MACU. That's just this street.

   EMILIA *relaxes.*

EMILIA. What did you get for Laura?

MACU. Oh! – I could give her these ankle-bracelets. Do you think?

EMILIA. See what I got her?

   A doll.

MACU. For Laura! She'd rather hit boys than play with dolls. – Was she alright last night?

EMILIA. Yes. Alright. She was talking in her sleep again. Shouting things: noises: like someone having a fit. Then she shouted: Stay still! Stay still! – Did he used to hit her?

MACU. No.

EMILIA. What then?

MACU. Nothing. He'd come in drunk and throw things at her. Or next morning when he wanted her to be quiet, he'd put a knife on the table between him and her and tell her not to move.

EMILIA. And why didn't you stop him?

MACU. It has gone quiet.

   WOCKY *and* LAURA *come on. They've been looting too.*

WOCKY. There you are. Where did you two get to?

MACU. Laura! How are you, pet?

WOCKY. She's in a huff. I told her off.

MACU. Why, what's she done this time?

WOCKY. She went for a big boy with a stone in her hand.

WOCKY *and* MACU *have a smile at this, strictly between them, before –*

MACU. That's wrong, I've told you that. Do you hear me?

WOCKY. That's her in a huff with you now.

MACU. You might hurt somebody. – So come here and see what I got you. Ankle bracelets.

LAURA. Ankle bracelets?

MACU. Do you not like them?

LAURA. What are they for?

MACU. You hang them from your ears, what do you *think* they're for?

EMILIA. Show her the other thing you got her. Look, Laura.

LAURA. A doll? Is it for me?

EMILIA. Here.

LAURA. Oh, she's lovely. Can I keep her?

EMILIA. Of course you can! We got it for you.

LAURA. Can I, mammy? Look: she's a beautiful black baby princess. Thanks, Emilia, that's the best thing anyone's ever given me. I'll make her clothes and look after her and everything, because look, she's only a baby and I don't want anything bad to happen to *her*. Guess what her name is, mammy.

MACU. What?

LAURA. Sharma.

MACU. Oh, that's a lovely name. And do you not want your ankle-bracelets? They're all the fashion, you'll look like a lady.

LAURA. Everyone will laugh at me.

MACU. More likely they'll laugh at your doll.

LAURA. Anyone laughs at her and I'll punch them one!

In a sudden loss of temper, MACU *hits her, or goes to hit her.*

MACU. Away inside and play with your doll then!

WOCKY. Macu!

LAURA *goes to exit then stops. She wants to make up to her mother for disappointing her. She holds up the ankle-bracelets.*

LAURA. Look, mammy – maybe these are really a necklace for my doll – see!

She exits.

MACU. Oh well! One of these days I'll do something right.

WOCKY. She's only eight, Macu.

MACU. I know that!

FLOOD *enters.*

FLOOD. Off the streets – quick – in.

EMILIA. Flood.

MACU. What is it?

FLOOD. Quick! Lepidus has left.

WOCKY. Left?

FLOOD. Rome! He stepped out of his bed this morning, splash into a puddle of blood. His three bodyguards had been killed in the night and hung up to bleed. And now there's dagger-men out on the streets, I watched some of them take a butcher's hand-saw and *saw a man's hand off* – for stealing.

EMILIA *starts to gather up her loot.*

EMILIA. Quick!

FLOOD. Leave that where it is. Come on.

MACU. Ahhhh, run then!

FLOOD. Why, what are you going to do?

MACU. I'm staying where I am.

FLOOD. It's over, Macu. In these contests the dead don't get buried, they get dumped in the Tiber with the bad meat. Emilia – go to Crassus, tell him we'll mourn for Sulla.

EMILIA *makes to go.*

MACU. Emilia!

EMILIA. No, Macu.

MACU. 'No, Macu' – what's this 'no, Macu'. I haven't said anything yet. – Do we even know who's behind this?

FLOOD. Some of them are saying it's Pompey. Does it matter?

MACU. Pompey? Oh panic then. Pompey? He's a boy!

EMILIA. Oh so you know Pompey. You can judge his character.

MACU. He's a people-pleaser! You've seen him in the Assembly. He got down on his knees and barked just to make people laugh.

EMILIA. Pompey? – you don't know your own daughter!

MACU. *I'm not mourning Sulla!* This voice is what I've got.

WOCKY. Macu!

MACU. This rusty razor I've got for a tongue! Nobody shuts *me* up, not any more.

FLOOD. On you go, Emilia.

MACU. And don't you dare say I don't know my own daughter, I have to sleep in the same bed as her half the time, it's me that gets her elbow in my face, I have to live with her!

YANIS *comes on.*

YANIS. Off the streets. They're coming.

EMILIA *and* FLOOD *go off in different directions.* MACU *shouts at them as they go* –

MACU. I can get to Pompey, don't you worry.

WOCKY *starts to go, backing away.*

WOCKY. Come on, Macu. We can shout about it later.

MACU. Yanis. You'll help me, won't you?

YANIS. Later, Macu.

MACU. Tonight. We'll do something tonight.

YANIS. Tonight.

YANIS *and* WOCKY *go.*

MACU. *I'm coming, Pompey!* I'm coming!

She goes.

Scene Six

Moonlit garden. POMPEY *comes on. This is the garden where last night he made his holy vow.*

POMPEY. Don't cry, Pompey, it's only the moon. You can't see the moon without wanting to fall on your knees and make a vow.

MARCELLA *comes on.*

MARCELLA. Pompey. Sorcha's here. Will I tell him you're out here in the garden?

POMPEY. How's Rome? Did he say?

MARCELLA. Quiet, he said.

POMPEY. What kind of quiet? Too quiet?

MARCELLA. Peaceful. The cafés are beginning to open up. People are talking about you. Drunken café talk.

POMPEY. Like what?

MARCELLA. They're making it up, most of it. Apparently, your father isn't your father, you're the secret offspring of a dark liaison between your mother and an Indian prince, which explains your jet-black shoulder-length hair. Don't worry, you can get a wig, and buy a pair of Indian slippers. – Everything's fine. The mob kicked someone's head off yesterday. People want peace again.

POMPEY. So long as the people know I didn't do this for the senate. I had personal reasons. – The people could have taken me apart today. They could have pulled me apart like a wishbone.

MARCELLA. They're calling you the young prince. You should be pleased. Who knows what they're calling me, the old slag probably. – So don't think so much.

They kiss. RANA *comes on.*

RANA. Pompey.

MARCELLA. Go away!

RANA. There's some mourners outside. They're wailing and laughing and holding up bits of dog – they've torn a dog apart with their hands and they're shouting things about your father. Listen.

MACU, WOCKY, YANIS *and some others come on and circle round the perimeter of the stage, as if round the outside of* POMPEY's *house. Again they use voice and primitive instruments to create unease.*

I've seen the wailers among the tombs, hurting themselves with stones and screaming swearwords at the gods. But when I saw them outside the house, I dropped.

MACU. Pompey's father.

YANIS. Giblets.

MACU. Pompey's dreams.

WOCKY. Giblets.

YANIS. Look, Pompey.

MACU. Remember your father's funeral? Remember bits of him got handed round the crowd?

YANIS. Recognise this bit?

MACU. Like father, like son.

POMPEY. Get me Sorcha. Quick.

RANA *goes.*

YANIS. Think about it, Pompey. You come apart over this and who'll put you together again?

MACU. What's Sulla to you?

YANIS. Make up your mind, Pompey. Who do you want to please?

MACU. Please the people, Pompey. We don't forget.

WOCKY. Macu, Yanis: that's enough. Let's go.

MACU. Pompey's father.

YANIS. Gibletsssss.

MACU. Pompey's dreams.

YANIS. Gibletsssss.

MACU. Night night, Pompey.

They exit.

POMPEY. Get me Sorcha. Quick.

MARCELLA. You sent Rana for him.

POMPEY. Get Rana then! Are you cold, I'm cold: it's that big, sad moon, it looks right through you.

SORCHA *arrives*.

SORCHA. Pompey.

POMPEY. Do we know where they live?

SORCHA. They all live in the same street. No one else wants to live with them.

POMPEY. Good. Do it then.

POMPEY *makes to exit*.

MARCELLA. Pompey. Speak to the senate first. Take your time.

POMPEY. I'm going to my room.

MARCELLA. The past is the past!

POMPEY. Please, Marcella! Don't involve me in this, don't make the same mistake they did! This is what makes me a general. When a battle starts I become someone else. I calculate. – I regret this action too, but I've given my word.

SORCHA. Pompey –

POMPEY. What?!

SORCHA. You haven't said what action you want me to take.

POMPEY. You decide. Don't report back. See that moon? I want to look out my window tonight and watch it turn red. I want fire.

POMPEY *goes*. SORCHA *makes to go in the other direction*.

MARCELLA. Sorcha.

This is a plea. SORCHA *goes*. MARCELLA *goes after* POMPEY.

Pompey! Pompey!

Scene Seven

Night. MACU *and* WOCKY *come on.* MACU *has been drinking.* WOCKY *is holding her by the arm.*

MACU. *I shut Pompey up! Me! Macu!* Where's Pompey's dagger-men now? Heh Flood: where's Pompey's dagger-men now? – Where are we? Where are you taking me?

WOCKY. Come on, we're nearly home.

MACU. I don't want to go home, I want to tell people what I've done.

WOCKY. You've been telling people all night. People are sleeping.

MACU. So wake the lazy bastards up!

WOCKY. Will you shhhh!

MACU. Don't 'shhhsh' me, who are you, my husband? Nobody gags me. And get your dirty hands off!

And she hits him. WOCKY *gets caught off balance and lands on the ground.*

WOCKY. I'm sick of you tonight! Fight? I've had to pull you out of two fights already, now you want to start one with me! I'm trying to help get you home in one piece, ya ugly cow! Did you leave your brains on a table somewhere?

The next thing MACU *says is quiet, defensive. The mouthful she's got off* WOCKY *has sobered her up.*

MACU. Just don't tell me to shut up ever. That's all he ever said to me.

WOCKY. I said 'Shhh'. I didn't slap you one in the mouth, I said 'Shhh'. And I have never told you to shut up.

MACU. Right. Calm down.

WOCKY. *Me* calm down? *I've* to calm down?

MACU. Shhhh. People are sleeping.

WOCKY. Don't 'shhhsh' me! *I'm calm.*

MACU *smiles.*

MACU. Come here and give me a kiss then.

WOCKY. What?

MACU. Come on. Make it up to me.

Pause. WOCKY *can't decide whether to laugh or slap her one.*

WOCKY. You defeat me.

MACU. On you go, smile.

WOCKY. I mean: *why?*

MACU. Why?

WOCKY. You. Me. You me. Why?

MACU. Because you're a good shag. Now stop playing for time and get over here before I change my mind.

Maybe she moves towards him.

WOCKY. You're some woman.

MACU. I know.

WOCKY. I should slap you in the mouth.

They hold each other. First they try a few tentative little kisses. Then they kiss. Then the kiss gets deep and sexy and urgent.

WOCKY. I want to wear your skin. I want you to tear my throat out.

They kiss again. Then part.

Can I come home with you?

MACU. I have to make it up with Laura.

There's a shout off, quite distant, of 'FIRE'.

WOCKY. Fuck.

MACU. I have to.

WOCKY. I know, I know.

MACU. She likes it when it's me and her alone.

WOCKY. Tomorrow then?

MACU. I'll see how she is.

Another shout: 'FIRE'. MACU and WOCKY hear it, but their first reactions are tentative.

MACU. Fire.

WOCKY. That's near our block.

Another shout: 'FIRE'.

WOCKY. That's near our block!

MACU. Quick. Run.

WOCKY. Come on.

MACU. I'm coming. Run!

WOCKY *goes.* MACU *looks in the direction of the fire a moment, then runs.*

Scene Eight

People come on carrying buckets of water etc. Shouting. MACU *enters. Then* YANIS *comes on dragging a soaked mattress.*

MACU. Yanis! Is everyone out?

YANIS. See that. Round the back, seven mattresses. Six went up: bonfire. One stayed dead. Look at that: one scorch mark where they flung the torch. Then the torch went out. Smell it: soaked in oil.

MACU. Oil.

YANIS. Sodden.

MACU. Pompey? Was this Pompey?

YANIS. We scared Pompey. Now he's scaring us.

YANIS *drags the mattress away.*

MACU. Someone pour oil on me. Someone put a light to me. – Wocky!

WOCKY *comes on.*

MACU. Did you see her?

WOCKY. No. Nobody's seen her.

MACU. Maybe she got out the back.

WOCKY. The whole rectangle's on fire, the whole island!

MACU. Maybe she's trapped out the back!

WOCKY. I'm going in.

WOCKY *exits in direction of fire.*

MACU. Laura! Laura!

EMILIA comes on, leading FLOOD *by the arm.* FLOOD *looks like she's walked out of the fire.*

FLOOD. You.

MACU. Flood.

FLOOD. Look at her. Not a finger on her. Not a mark. See these?

She holds out her badly burned hands.

– stumps!

MACU. I never thought . . .

FLOOD. You never thought!

MACU. You warned me.

FLOOD. I warned you! No hands. What do I need hands for now – I've no husband.

MACU. No husband?

FLOOD. No hands. No husband. I wish you were dead.

MACU. What have I been thinking about?

FLOOD. Not us. Not us.

FLOOD turns and exits.

MACU. What have I done? I just followed my tongue, I had a rusty brown razor in my mouth. O God, did I do wrong? I don't want anything now. I just want Laura. I just want Wocky. Yes, I'll cry for Sulla, of course I will, I'll give it throat, lungs, here, from right down here! I just want Laura. I just want Wocky.

EMILIA. Macu. Here's Wocky coming now.

WOCKY walks on. He's got LAURA's *doll, nothing else. The fire's begun to die down.*

MACU. Wocky.

WOCKY. This is all I could find.

The doll. He doesn't know what to do with it.

EMILIA. You're all burnt.

WOCKY. Burnt . . . am I? Not enough.

EMILIA. Your clothes.

WOCKY. Clothes. Just my stupid clothes.

MACU. Is she dead?

WOCKY. You go to my house. I'll stay here and look.

MACU. Is she dead? I *slept* with her last night. Not last night the night before last, the night before last. She was all clammy. So I wet a towel and wiped her face, then her neck, then her chest, then her belly, then her legs, then back again. And now – she grew two inches this year – and now –

EMILIA. Come on we'll go, Macu.

EMILIA *starts to lead her away.* MACU *goes with her, obediently.*

MACU. She'll have got out somehow. Because what was the point of her growing two inches, if she was just going to . . .

EMILIA. Come on just now.

MACU. I was on my way back. I promised her I'd be home. I was looking forward to it, just me and her alone. – Oh Laura . . . if I'd been a good mother, I'd be dead by now. I'd have been there.

MACU *and* EMILIA *go off, holding onto each other. From off – the sound of wailing, tentative, frightened, not yet full-throated.* WOCKY *exits.*

Scene Nine

EMILIA *enters.*
Then WOCKY. *He's dragging charred timbers from the burnt-out fire.*

EMILIA. Find anything?

WOCKY. No.

EMILIA. Don't look any more, Wocky. You've looked for two days.

WOCKY *holds out the doll.*

WOCKY. What will I do with this?

EMILIA. Do *you* want it?

WOCKY. Yes.

EMILIA. Keep it then.

WOCKY. Then Macu would see it.

Pause.

EMILIA. Sulla's funeral this afternoon. – How's Macu?

WOCKY. Burning hot plate, doesn't tell you it's hot.

EMILIA. What?

WOCKY. Then you pick it up.

EMILIA. Should someone not be with her?

WOCKY. She sleeps on the other side of the room. Say goodnight to her and she – hisses.

EMILIA. Hisses?

WOCKY. Tsssst! – I walk into the room and she doesn't see me. Touch her and she looks at me like I've flicked hot oil in her face. Does she blame *me?* Then I woke up this morning and she's sitting on a chair wearing her dead clothes, ready for this afternoon.

EMILIA. She's doing the funeral then?

WOCKY. Yes.

EMILIA. Are you?

He shrugs.

EMILIA. Have you seen the streets? There's thousands of them lining the route already, five deep, three miles either side the road. I've never seen so many.

WOCKY. So we were a minority then.

EMILIA. Looks like it. – I have to go get ready now. How about you?

Pause.

WOCKY. I'll see how I feel.

EMILIA *goes.*
WOCKY *buries the doll under some rubble, and builds a little burial mound.*

WOCKY. Remember I caught you fighting that boy? He was lucky
I stopped you: mess? he'd a face like a burst orange. And then
you went for him with a stone in your hand. Rage. – And you
were so stubborn, like your mother. Then the other day, when
you took my hand? Neither of us looked at each other, I was
scared to look at you, in case you pulled your hand away again.
So I just walked along, holding this tiny hot hand, this child.
And then, after a good long while, I looked at you. Your wee
old face. Your old, old, old, wee face. – You were lovely, Laura.

EMILIA *and* MACU *come on, both wearing their dead clothes.*

EMILIA. Wocky. We're going now.

WOCKY. When will we cry?

EMILIA. You'd better come if you're coming.

MACU *and* EMILIA *go.*

WOCKY. When will we cry?

WOCKY *exits.*

Scene Ten

*Noise off of mourners wailing a funeral chant. All very Arabic in feel.
Then* WOCKY *comes on.*

WOCKY. Thousands of them. – What are you looking at? What
are you looking at? – Thirty, forty deep, jammed sideways on
balconies. Oh Sulla, our lungs are hot, necks tight, throats
swollen, a hundred thousand of us, more, silent, welded
together. And listen to that –

Wailing off.

Does that not scratch your blood? Cover Laura's ears someone.
O God, put your hands over Laura's ears, don't let her hear
grief like this. And here it comes, here comes the rain, even the
sky's shedding tears. Ah why not, cry for Sulla, cry for Sulla,
everyone else is: that woman's nose is weeping, that man's scar
is weeping, that's not the rain running down her face, there are
thoughts in her heart, Sulla, tears in her eyes, the whole world's
thinking of you.

He starts to back off, away from the oncoming procession.

Our lungs are hot, necks tight, throats swollen and here they come, here they come, here they come.

He either exits or hides, before —
The MOURNERS *enter.*
And wail. However formally this may be staged, the intention should be to achieve a primitive expression of grief, which fills the entire stage.

When they exit, they leave behind a very empty stage.

WOCKY *walks back into the middle of it.*

WOCKY. Grief. Grief. Grief.

He pulls something over his head. His shirt, or some rags he finds. Then he lies down. He wants to hide. He wants to curl up and die.

Scene Eleven

MACU *comes on. She's come from the funeral.*

WOCKY. Macu.

MACU. You.

WOCKY. Is that it over?

MACU. Were you watching?

WOCKY. Yes.

MACU. You? – Remember that day? I wore my veil of flame orange, you threw nuts to the children; and everyone made the usual jokes. I hope your nuts don't rattle like that ha ha. When *I* do it *she* hears castanets ha ha.

WOCKY. Macu. Don't blame yourself.

MACU. And I wanted all that. The sweet smiling children, the dirty rattle of castanets at night, I wanted all that.

WOCKY. Why blame yourself, because of the fire? That was Pompey.

MACU. Tsssst!

WOCKY. Pompey had a tantrum, burst into flames.

MACU. Tsssshhhht!

WOCKY. It's Pompey –

MACU. *I blame you, that's who I blame!* Coming home drunk throwing knives at her. Throwing knives at her and looking at me to see what I'd do. What was I supposed to do? So then I'm left with her. And I don't even like her by then, she's a tribe of monkeys jumping all over me, fits and tantrums and fights, a tribe of monkeys! – Then I take you back.

WOCKY. Macu. This is Wocky.

MACU. Then I take you back.

WOCKY. Wocky, Wocky, Wocky, Wocky!

Pause.

MACU. I think I'll go. Lie in ditches. Eat moths. Get lost.

She goes.

WOCKY. Yes. That's one way to put out a fire. Demolish everything round about. – So one day I'll see a woman, washing her hair in a stream. I'll fall in love with her. I'll throw a stone in the water. She'll turn and smile and I'll ask her her name and then we'll get married. – Because what's wrong with that? – Macu! – Never fall in love with someone whose heart is broken. They'll break your heart.

He goes.

Scene Twelve

Shrine in a wood.

A woman enters. Places fruit at altar. Offers incense.

RANEE. You'll have heard the news by now I take it. Sulla got his funeral. – The man with the pus-sy eye that works in the women's baths and scalded my belly that time with the boiling jug of water for no earthly reason that I could see except that he's a bad bastard: he told me. Then he gave me one of his smirks. Only he's got an infection of the mouth just now so he just looked stupid. I said to him, what's wrong with your mouth, is that thrush you've got? – I was right too. – Now Lepidus has raised an army up north, he's marching on Rome;

only, Pompey has raised another army army up north and he's marching on Lepidus. They say Lepidus is seven days ahead. – Thank you for the day. More people came to me today, to be healed. Two of them had nothing wrong with them so that was easy enough. Then there was the two who had devils in them. Then a woman who had burned her hands and couldn't hold things. So I healed her and cast out the two devils then I went to the baths. – I love woods. Even in spring, dead leaves: soft, thick rot. And the quiet. Like the whole wood is listening. When a bird sings you can hear every note . . . the pauses. One day I'll come here, bury myself under the dead leaves and die. – They say it's only half-witted gods like the Vetch that live in the woods, the important ones all have their temples in the city. They say all kinds of rubbish, they don't even listen to it themselves. I come and pray in secret because you live in secret, like the healing plants, you wait for me. – I saw the Vetch today. There's a god and a half: big, and stupid with it. He'd a big shaggy tree over his shoulder, he'd pulled it out of the ground like a vegetable, roots and all and he was off to plant it somewhere else. He likes that. He moves a tree from one part of the wood to another then the next day he moves it back again. – I'll go now. – Oh, the two devils. One was called Hista and one was called Geb. I drove them into some black rocks.

Exits.

Scene Thirteen

Enter SIZE. *He's a mule-driver.*

SIZE. *Move it. Keep those beasts moving. Hit it then! Hit the thing. Of course it's stubborn, it's a mule: beat its brains out with a rock.*
Awffa. Dust.
Come on, come on, let's keep this army moving. Lorca. Haw – Lorca.
Because the animal's lying down, you don't have to lie down with it. What? I can *see* it's dying, so what's the problem, is it a brother of yours? Break its legs and move on.

An OFFICER *has entered.*

Come on, come on, keep it going. Move it, move it, *move it.*

OFFICER. That's it. Call a halt. We're stopping.

The OFFICER *has gone.*

SIZE. *Halt. Halt, I said. Let's get this army halted.* Blebbo. Blebbo! Break its bastarding legs then, that'll stop it.

He turns away from some offensive offstage pile-up, covering his face.

I give up. That's right, fall on top of each other, *bury each other. Now make camp,* before I choke.

GRIN *comes on. He's a soldier.*

GRIN. Hear the news, we've halted. Four miles from Rome (give me some water my *balls* are aching) four miles from Rome. Lepidus wants us to halt here till Rome (something or other), till the people –

SIZE. Till the people what?

GRIN. What? (My balls are bursting) till the people –

SIZE. Till the people what?

GRIN. (How long have I got to get my hole?) I don't know, do I! – (rise up). How far behind us is Pompey?

SIZE. Five days.

GRIN. Five days? Yooh! *I want my fanny and I want it raw!* Have you seen her, have you seen her?

SIZE. Seen who?

GRIN. Who? My aching balls, that's who. Macu. Her that wandered into camp looking like a leper.

SIZE. She'd been eating twigs. What's your excuse?

GRIN. Haw. So everyone else looked at her and it put them off their rations So I take her bits of meat every day, figs. You should see her now: gratitude?: she's barking for it. – Fancy it then? Haw. Fancy a bit of nasty? Because five days.

SIZE. What, you want me to come with you?

GRIN. You could hold her down. – I've only got five days or I wouldn't ask you.

SIZE. Grin. Can I give you some counsel? Desert. Sneak back to Rome. You've been sleeping next to me for thirty long cold nights and I haven't been tempted once. So if that's *me*, how's a woman going to feel? Because they're not like us, they like to get some pleasure from it.

GRIN. Haw.

SIZE. I'm going to wash, eat something.

SIZE *exits. Once he's safely gone,* GRIN *spits, as if he's intending to hit* SIZE, *then exits.*

Scene Fourteen

WOCKY *enters. Then* BUTTER.

WOCKY. Can you help me?

BUTTER. I see, I see.

WOCKY. I'm looking for a woman.

BUTTER. Woman woman woman, all the men are down at the river swimming. I get thirsty, just looking at them, because fair enough that's two days we've been camped here. What's a vote?

WOCKY. A vote?

BUTTER. Is it? I see, I see.

WOCKY. It's when –

BUTTER. Right right, I get it now.

WOCKY. I haven't said what it is yet, mothbrain.

BUTTER. I see, I see. So how do you do that with your feet? Is it like thingmy, kick. You vote some poor prick's head in. Because I heard this man saying the soldiers are voting with their feet. And likes of, know how they gave me a right good voting yesterday, I thought I'd keep the old head down.

WOCKY. Can you not run away?

BUTTER. I see, I see.

SIZE *appears.*

SIZE. Leave the boy alone you. – So what's this, another one out from Rome? How are things there, quiet? I'll bet they are. Because all the riff-raff's here! Army camp? It's more like a fair. When Lepidus asked you to join us he didn't mean come and have a holiday! – On you go, Butter: exit.

BUTTER *exits*.

WOCKY. I'm looking for a woman. She's called Macu. I heard a rumour she was a baggage-carrier.

Slight pause.

SIZE. Can I give you some counsel? Go home. She's a baggage-carrier. I can't put it any plainer than that.

WOCKY. So she's here? You know her?

SIZE. Look. You tell me she's a baggage-carrier: I'm explaining, your woman's a baggage-carrier, then you should go home. They come, something bad's happened to them. So then they're here, worse things happen. They're women. – When there's a battle they get drunk on some brew and go up a hill to watch. What a laugh they have. Some poor soldier catches a spear in his throat and they roll around eating the dust.

WOCKY. Where is she? I know someone, can get her better.

SIZE. Go home. Nobody gets better.

SIZE *goes. Then* WOCKY.

Scene Fifteen

Evening, but still light. OOLA *and* JALATA *carry* AYEESHA *on, on a stretcher.* AYEESHA *has passed out drunk.*

OOLA. Hurry up, I want to get back to the men.

They put the stretcher down.

JALATA. Help me lie her down on the grass, Oola.

OOLA. Drunk cow. How many men has she had today?

JALATA. Three. Each one a different colour.

OOLA. Yuch! That can't have done her baby any good.

They lie her down on the grass. JALATA *slaps her on the face.*

JALATA. Ayeesha! Ayeesha!

OOLA. I'm beginning to wonder if she wants her baby.

MACU *and* ZUZIBARRA *come on, with* GRIN *trailing after them.*

MACU. Oola. Where's the drink?

OOLA. Where's the men?

MACU. We left them there. Where's the drink?

OOLA. I gave the last bottle to the young one with the moustache.

MACU. He said that was his.

As MACU *exits to investigate.*

OOLA. Oh no, don't tell me.

ZUZIBARRA. What?

MACU *comes back.*

MACU. The men have fucked off with the drink.

Only ZUZIBARRA *is shocked.*

I told you to stay with them, Zuzi!

GRIN. You've still got me. Because I'm not fussy, I want my fanny and I want it raw.

GRIN's *a man and* GRIN's *got a bottle.*

MACU. What's your name again?

GRIN. Grin.

MACU. I'm Macu. Come here and give me a kiss then.

OOLA. What about us?

MACU. You can watch.

MACU *takes a bottle off* GRIN *and has a drink.*

Come on then, ugly. Open up.

They kiss. OOLA, JALATA *and* ZUZIBARRA *watch.*

OOLA. Jalata. Come here and give me a kiss.

JALATA. No. I can't kiss you, I *know* you.

OOLA. What about you, Zuzi?

ZUZIBARRA. I'm watching them.

GRIN *and* MACU *part.* GRIN *needs air,* MACU *needs drink.*

GRIN. Will we go and find a field? Somewhere on our own.

MACU *pushes him over, without even looking at him.*

MACU. You go. Find yourself a dead sheep, so you won't break its heart. What happened to the boy with the lovely slim legs, me and him were getting on great. Lovely young thing, smelled as sweet as a baby's head, where did he get to?

ZUZIBARRA. You pushed him in the river. Laugh? – he broke his arm.

MACU. I liked him.

SIZE *enters.*

SIZE. Have you heard the news? Pompey's only two days march away: he's been marching them through the nights.

Vast indifference. MACU *goes to sit on the vacant stretcher.*

ZUZIBARRA. Two days march? How long will that take them?

OOLA. Ahch – ages.

MACU. Have you got any drink?

SIZE. Two days, soldier.

SIZE *goes. – At different points in the scene, each of the women has run out of drunken energy. Each is now lost in her own world. We have no idea whether they're thinking deep thoughts or even if they're thinking at all. They're just very far away.*

GRIN. Jalata. How about you and me go and find a field? Two days is all I've got. Fancy it?

She doesn't hear him.

Oola, how about you and me go and find a field? Because two days. Oola.

OOLA. Shhh, I'm thinking.

GRIN. Zuzi. Two days and I'm manure. I'm next year's crops.

ZUZIBARRA. I was just looking at those crops there. What are they?

ZUZI *looks at the crops.* OOLA *thinks.* GRIN *gives up.* JALATA *looks at the sky. A bird stops singing. Then* MACU *lies back on the stretcher and crosses her arms over her chest.*

MACU. Bury me. Bury me. Carry me through the streets like a queen, coldly beautiful. Carry me through the streets at night. The moon will be white, my face will be white (the sun's a vulture, the sun's a flesh-eater) the moon, the moon's lovely, like a good mother, watching quietly from far away.

OOLA, JALATA *and* ZUZI *think this is beautiful. Like a beautiful fairy-tale.*

OOLA. Oh.

ZUZIBARRA. Look at her. Arms crossed.

JALATA. Coldly beautiful.

OOLA. I want to be coldly beautiful.

MACU. Line the streets for me and sigh as I pass. And I'll leave you behind, mourning and wailing in this vale of tears –

JALATA. Lift her up.

MACU. – mourning and weeping in this valley of sorrows. Sing a sad song. Sing a song of longing for the Libyan queen.

They lift her up on the stretcher and carry her around the stage, wailing sadly.

WOCKY *enters and watches.*

WOCKY. Macu! Macu!

MACU *can't hear him over the singing, but* JALATA *and* OOLA *hear him – and the wailing trails off.* WOCKY *motions them to put the stretcher down, which they do.*

OOLA. There's someone to see you, Macu.

MACU. Tell them I'm dead.

WOCKY. Macu.

She rises up.

MACU. Wocky.

WOCKY. Death, what's death? You only die once. Don't listen to me, my brain's –. Are you listening to me? Rome's –

He wants to say, 'Rome's empty without you'.

Will you come back to me? – Ho. I want to get *you* better? I'm worse than you. I die thirty times a day. Every time I put food

in my mouth I want to cry. – I passed through the field there.
See all the dead bodies? Well they're only drunk. Look: him:
fat old boy, face like a red cabbage. What a thirst he'll wake up
with. And there's a young courting couple laughing at him. – I
want to be them. That couple. Can we be them?

MACU. How did you find me?

WOCKY. You were only –

MACU. *Will you two stop sniggering?*

Nobody's sniggering.

WOCKY. – four miles away.

Beat.

MACU. So, how's Emilia?

WOCKY. Good.

MACU. How's Flood?

WOCKY. Better.

MACU. Better?

WOCKY. Better than she was.

Beat.

MACU. Do you see my friends? This is Jalata. This is Oola. And
that's Ayeesha lying on the grass. She's going to have a baby.

ZUZIBARRA. Waaaaaaah!

MACU. That's Zuzi laughing. She's got the brains of a dogfish. –
So here we are, take your pick, which one do you want? We're
all a scream.

Beat.

WOCKY. There's a woman. Ranee. She remembers the old gods,
the gods of the country. She goes round the villages, healing
people and casting out devils. I went and saw her. I told her all
about you. She says she can make you better. – First Emilia
went to her. Then Flood. Flood can use her hands again. Her
hands were like that: dead: Emilia had to feed her. Then she
went to Ranee. Ranee took her hands and said, there's nothing
wrong with your hands. Flood cried till she was empty and the
next day her hands were better.

OOLA. Oh.

MACU. She opened her hands?

WOCKY. She looks you in the eye again.

OOLA. Could she make me better? I want to be better.

MACU. And she made Flood better?

WOCKY. She still cries, she still remembers.

MACU. But she's better?

WOCKY. Yes.

Pause, as MACU *tries to remember what being better would be like, how things used to be.*

MACU. Remember the day (look at me now!) who was there that day? And say I went to see her, then what?

WOCKY. Come back to Rome. Come back to me. – All the bad things have already happened, Macu, only good things can happen now. And I want you, Macu. So you've a bad temper, so what? I'm ugly. – Then later on, we could maybe have a baby. – Go and see Ranee. Please.

Beat.

MACU. Better. – And can she make Pompey better?

WOCKY. Pompey?

MACU. You don't know who Pompey is?

WOCKY. Pompey? What's he got to do with it?

MACU. So forget it then! It was you that brought it up. – So say we have a baby. What will we *call* her?

WOCKY. There's lots of names.

MACU. Pompeia?

WOCKY. Macu. I know what he did and –

MACU. So you remember him?

WOCKY. *So Pompey!* So what are you going to do about it? Memorise his name? Because if you can't do anything about it, then –

MACU. What can I do? Nothing!

WOCKY. – then leave it. Don't torment yourself.

MACU. I'll print myself on Pompey's heart like an inscription on a tomb!

Beat.

WOCKY. Rhetoric. You're good at that. What about my heart? What about this tomb?

SIZE *enters.*

SIZE. Move it. We're retreating.

ZUZIBARRA. Oh, quick, where?

SIZE. Quick: everyone's all over the place. Army?

JALATA. What's the panic?

SIZE. See that dirty big cloud lying over yonder. It's not a cloud.

GRIN *and* MACU *move downstage to look out front at* POMPEY's *dirty big army advancing on them. A moment of silence, then –*

MACU. Pompey.

GRIN. Pompey.

SIZE. So come on now, move it! – That's you, Grin, you've had your time.

SIZE *goes.* GRIN *goes too, almost in tears, and chucking his last semi-hysterical lines at the women.*

GRIN. Five days! Now do you see? I only had five days! Crops!

As the women get ready to go, WOCKY *and* MACU *face each other.*

WOCKY. Macu. What about this heart? What about your heart?

MACU *looks at him. Maybe she'll go with him. Then –*

MACU. Blame Pompey.

WOCKY *grabs her and tries to kiss her. She pushes him away. They struggle with each other. He gets her on the ground and sits on her. He wants to hit her. Maybe he makes to hit her. Then he screams at her. Then he gets up and goes. She sits up.*

OOLA. What will we do with Ayeesha? Macu, what will we do with Ayeesha?

MACU. Put her on the stretcher. You'll have to carry her.

JALATA. Where are *you* going?

MACU. I'm going to find Pompey.

OOLA *looks at her.* JALATA *goes over to try and shift* AYEESHA.

JALATA. Will you help me, Oola? This obstinate cow won't shift.

OOLA *goes to her and helps her lift* AYEESHA *onto the stretcher.*

ZUZIBARRA. We'll have to get Ayeesha some oranges. Look at her skin! Blood oranges. That's what my mother gave me when I was pregnant. She said it was good for the blood or the baby or something.

JALATA *stops to look at* MACU, *who's still sitting where she was.*

JALATA. Are you coming?

There's no answer. OOLA *and* JALATA *carry the stretcher off, followed by* ZUZIBARRA.

MACU *looks around. She makes to exit. She's not very sure where to go. She doesn't go in the same direction as* OOLA. *Nor does she go in the direction of* POMPEY's *army. She wanders off, lost, into the wilderness.*

ACT TWO

Scene One

The sea. PHYLLIDA *and* NUDDY *come on. They've been gathering sea-weed, and now they want a rest.*

NUDDY. Isn't the sea sad, bie? I see the sea and I want to sit down girl, and have a good cry. All my life – sea. I might as well live in a boat. And do I get used to it? No. I come outside, bie – tears!

Silence. They watch the sea.

PHYLLIDA. Look who's coming, Nuddy.

MACU *comes on. She's been sleeping rough these last few months. Also, she looks pregnant. Sometimes she strokes her belly absently but gently. Sometimes she punches at it absently but hard.* PHYLLIDA *and* NUDDY *watch her.*

PHYLLIDA. Let's get back to the field, girl.

NUDDY. There's no harm in her, Phyllida.

PHYLLIDA *strokes her belly.*

PHYLLIDA. I've a little sailor in here. Why does she hit herself?

NUDDY. Oh girl!

PHYLLIDA. I don't like her. What's she got in her belly, if she's feared of it?

NUDDY. I'm going to talk to her.

PHYLLIDA. I'm going, girl.

NUDDY. I'm only going to talk to her, no harm.

NUDDY *approaches* MACU *cautiously, keeping a distance.*

NUDDY. Today's the day, girl! We spread the sea-weed today. We manure the six fields. Then tonight!

PHYLLIDA. We light the bonfire tonight.

NUDDY. Oh there will be dancing and drinking tonight, bie, don't you believe it! There will be sad songs tonight.

PHYLLIDA. The young men will be gods tonight, bullocks, bie. So *she* hopes.

NUDDY. No I don't. No I don't, girl.

MACU *punches herself in the belly.*

What you got in there then, lucky girl? You don't want it you give it to me, lucky girl.

PHYLLIDA. You wouldn't!

NUDDY. I'm only joking, girl. (*I've got tits same as you, girl!*) – What you got in there then? Don't you be hurting the little sailor, or it'll split you open like a slaughtered cow. Don't you want it then?

MACU. Wocky wants it.

NUDDY. What's she saying?

MACU. Wocky wants it.

NUDDY. If you don't want it, we'se could take you to a woman.

PHYLLIDA. Oh – gaaaah! – that's bigger than mine is!

NUDDY. Let's take a look then, girl. Let's see how big it is.

When NUDDY *reaches out to touch* MACU, MACU *flinches away. So then* NUDDY *reaches out more slowly and touches* MACU's *hair, neck. She touches her very gently and beautifully.* MACU *surrenders to the touch completely. She makes a little noise, of pleasure.*

NUDDY. There you are now. Let's take a look then.

NUDDY *lays* MACU *down and unbuttons her to take a look at her baby.*

MACU. Is it, is it? And what will happen to it then? Because I was walking through the wood and a bird fell out of a tree: dumff!: right at my feet: then it swam across some stones and died? So I sat down and cried. Two days I sat for, then it came to life and flew away again. – Will I show you my trick? Who's got a walnut, oh I have.

During this, the 'baby' is uncovered. It's a stone. It's as if in her madness MACU's *been compelled to act out whether or not she wanted to have* WOCKY's *baby. So she put a stone down her skirt, which in*

time became her wanted/unwanted baby. – Now the stone is revealed,
she looks at it in bemusement.

Oh.

NUDDY. Oh girl.

NUDDY *lifts the stone off her belly and puts it on the ground.*

PHYLLIDA. Oh girl.

MACU. Wocky wanted it.

NUDDY. Oh girl. You're no more pregnant than I am.

MACU. Wocky wanted it.

NUDDY. You've no more in your belly than I have. You need a
man girl, same as I do. Oh bie.

PHYLLIDA. Don't touch her, Nuddy, she's a confusion! I've a
little sailor in here, why'd she put a stone down her skirt? She
put a stone down her skirt! She pretends she's got a baby in
her, then she punches the poor thing witless! Aiii, I'm going up
the field now, I am. I'm going up the field. – Are you coming?

NUDDY. You go then. I'll come later.

PHYLLIDA *comes back to try and scare* MACU *away.*

PHYLLIDA. You go. You go. I'll bring the others back with me,
won't I.

Then she goes.

NUDDY. Isn't the sea sad, bie? I see the sea and I want to sit
down girl, and have a good cry. – Come on then: I'll take you
somewhere safe. I'll bring you food later. We kill a beast
tonight. Some of the beast we throw on the bonfire, as an
offering. And the rest of it we roast. We bless the fields
tonight. The young men are bullocks, bie. – Leave the baby.

MACU *has bent down to pick up the stone. She stops for a moment,*
thinks about leaving it, but can't. She picks it up, confused now.

Come on then.

They go.

Scene Two

SORCHA *comes on and sets up a camp-stool.* POMPEY *comes on and sits on it. When he's ready,* SORCHA *begins his report.*

SORCHA. We've confirmed that Lepidus escaped by ship, probably to Sicily.

POMPEY *bounces up and starts walking up- and down-stage.*

Total casualities over the whole campaign: twenty-six. Enemy casualties: two hundred and forty two. The officers report –

POMPEY. Any word from Rome?

SORCHA. The senate's sending Crassus out to speak to you. Apparently Marcella's with him.

Pause. POMPEY *feels nauseous, though he may try and conceal this.*

POMPEY. Tell Marcella I'm sick. – And what will the predictable bastards offer me, do you think?

SORCHA. There's the war in Spain. They'll probably offer you the command.

POMPEY. Spain? Spain?

He says this with considerable disgust.
A young OFFICER *comes on, breathless.*

OFFICER. Pompey. Crassus and Marcella are here.

Pause.

POMPEY. Who's the *cheery* cunt? Tell him to go away, Sorcha.

The OFFICER *looks at* SORCHA. *Should he go?*

OFFICER. What will I say to Crassus?

POMPEY. Sorcha. Tell the young officer cunt to go away, recover his breath, and come back like he's got foot-rot.

The OFFICER *exits. Then enters again.*

OFFICER. Pompey.

POMPEY. Yes.

OFFICER. Crassus and Marcella are here.

POMPEY. *Go and get them then!*

The OFFICER *starts to go, fast.*

POMPEY. Oi!

The OFFICER *stops.*

POMPEY. Tell Marcella I've changed. Prepare her for the worst. Try and depress her a bit.

The OFFICER *goes.*

SORCHA. The quarter-master would like to know –

POMPEY. Why am I like this?

SORCHA. Like what?

POMPEY. Charmless. Boring. Brutal.

SORCHA. You're a soldier. You don't want to go home, that's all.

CRASSUS *and* MARCELLA *enter and stop.*

MARCELLA. Pompey.

POMPEY. Marcella.

MARCELLA'*s waiting for a sign from* POMPEY. *If he opened his arms she'd go to him. He doesn't.*

And how's Crassus?

MARCELLA. What kept you so long? You've been away for months.

POMPEY *laughs.*

POMPEY. What can I say? Lepidus gave me a lesson in generalship. I tried to think how he might think, get inside my opponent's mind. But he was ready for me, he kept his mind a complete blank. He'd stop his men and face me. Then just when I'd sorted out my battle-order, he'd retreat. Obviously, I'd hang back to see what the trick was. No trick. Four times he did that. Never have a battle of wits with someone who's stupid, they'll win every time. – So!

MARCELLA. So! Do I look older? It's your own fault for taking so long! I dyed my hair. But then I dyed it back again.

POMPEY. And? Is that it? 'I dyed my hair and then I dyed it back again.'

MARCELLA. I didn't want to shock you.

POMPEY. So. What's the talk in Rome?

CRASSUS. Put it this way. The senate asked me to kneel to you.

POMPEY. Oh? Good.

CRASSUS. They want to offer you the command in Spain.

Pause.

POMPEY. Ask Sorcha how my soldiers are, Crassus, I doubled
their pay last week, double it again, Sorcha. How are my
soldiers?

SORCHA. Happy.

POMPEY. Because I don't want to repeat myself, Crassus, and –
will someone please surprise me – I don't want to repeat myself –

MARCELLA. Are you sick?

POMPEY. – I don't want to repeat myself –

MARCELLA. His eyes are epileptic, Sorcha!

POMPEY. – *this is Pompey talking* – tell the senate: I want Rome to
give me a Triumph.

Beat.

MARCELLA. Am I the only one that can talk back to him?

CRASSUS. So you want to parade through Rome and display –
what?

POMPEY. Yes!

CRASSUS. You haven't captured a foreign country, Pompey, you
haven't plundered some foreign king, you haven't captured
exotic-looking women. So you have a Triumph, who are you
going to parade as prisoners? Romans?

POMPEY. No listen, Crassus, don't say any more, because I'll tell
you one of the reasons we can't communicate: life's too short.
You look at me and you see, who knows what you see, a young
man. So I'm twenty five, twenty six, *whatever*, I've got an
imagination: I'm nearly sixty. So that's one reason. Are you
keeping up?

He drums at his head with his fingertips.

It's too crowded in here. That's another reason. So now you're
all looking at me and Crassus is thinking – Pompey? – a paper

fire, a tantrum for a minute, then it's out. Because did I miss something, is there another army around I haven't been told about? I've got a happy army at my back, what have you got, Crassus? So don't tell me what size I am or who did I conquer, the people don't care who I conquered, all they want to see is a conqueror! – So it was a civil war. So it makes me sick too. So what?

Pause.

CRASSUS. I'll let the senate know what you have in mind.

He goes.

POMPEY. Sorcha. Speak to the quartermaster. Double the soldier's pay. I'm going to my tent.

He goes.

SORCHA. He's a good general. The men love him.

MARCELLA. Sorcha. He's only a boy. He's too young for you. – Does he know?

SORCHA. No.

MARCELLA. That's sad.

SORCHA. I have to go and see the quartermaster now.

MARCELLA. You're the same as me then. Well, he knows about me, I don't know if that makes it worse or better. You look so desolate. Is that how I look? I never want to look as *silent* as you do. – Can you show me back, I don't think I can find it.

She goes. Then SORCHA.

Scene Three

WOCKY *enters. He sits with his back to a wall. He's got a knife, which he's playing with. Maybe we should see he has a vague thought somewhere of using the knife, but this should only emphasise the vagueness.*
YANIS *comes on. He goes down on his hunkers close to the wall.*

YANIS. So we've got a new cunt on our hands. The late cunt only got torched six months ago and already some cunt's coming the cunt. And then they turn round and tell you you've a limited vocabulary. Bastards. – *Today* the cunt comes.

WOCKY. Listen. I'm going for a wander, Yanis. I'll see you later.

As WOCKY *goes.*

YANIS. No problem. I'll talk to myself.

SHARMA *enters backwards, shouting at someone off. She's got a stool, scissors, barber equipment.*

SHARMA. Ah get lost – take your customers? – what customers?? You don't call him a customer. Look at him, he's as bald as a wee boy's balls. Don't even talk to me! See your breath, it's like someone's opened a stank. If I had breath like you, I'd suffocate: I'd be frightened to open my mouth!

Then she sees YANIS.

YANIS. Will you do my hair?

SHARMA. No. Get lost. I only do people's hair that I like.

She chases YANIS *off. Then she sets up her stool etc.*
WOCKY *comes back, walking close to a wall.*

SHARMA. Wocky! You don't know me, my name's Sharma. I know you though. I don't *know* you, but I asked someone what your name was. Can I cut your hair?

WOCKY. Hair?

She takes the stool over to him.

SHARMA. I won't charge you. I'm not a proper barber, if any of them see me they chase me. I do my young brother's though! He's good-looking too. So don't argue. Come on: sit!

She's brought the stool behind him, and she bangs him in the leg with it to make him sit. Which he does.

So what would you like me to do? I could dye it. Only I don't have any dye. I'll trim it then. Relax, look at your shoulders, lean back. Don't talk to me or I can't concentrate (close your eyes) so I'll do all the talking I talk non-stop, my young brother's a dummy can't talk just makes these ohyoyoyo noises, so if I don't keep talking maybe I'll forget how and end up like him, (will I?)

Suddenly she stops and holds his head.

So listen: because you look so sad all the time: (I love you): so how's that?: that's you done. You have to get up now, I need my stool, it's not even *mine!*

Pause, as WOCKY *tries to catch up with her, and thinks about getting off the stool.*

WOCKY. What's your name?

SHARMA. I told you! Sharma.

WOCKY. Sharma. Are you annoyed with me?

SHARMA. I gave you your chance and you didn't take it.

WOCKY. When?

SHARMA. Then! Don't pretend you didn't hear. I came right out and told you everything. – Did you like it when I touched your head. You made a noise like you liked it.

WOCKY. You've got lovely small hands.

SHARMA. Well then?

Beat.

WOCKY. You're a soul.

SHARMA. What's that supposed to mean?

WOCKY. Nothing. It means, I hope everything turns out good for you.

SHARMA. Thanks.

She says 'thanks' like it means 'fuck off and die', and makes to exit.

WOCKY. Will you still talk to me?

SHARMA. I'll have to think about it.

She exits, with all her barber gear.

WOCKY. Because I like you.

She's gone. WOCKY *holds his head, where she held it. It's been a long time since anyone touched him.*

And I can't talk to the rest of them. I have conversations with dead people. I walk through the streets and I could nearly cry. All these ghosts yelling at one another, shouting, selling. They don't have mouths they have holes.

FLOOD enters.

FLOOD. Wocky.

WOCKY. Flood.

FLOOD. I've seen Macu.

WOCKY. Macu. Where?

FLOOD. Near where the fire was. There was a crowd round her. She's cut herself all over with a razor, thousands of tiny cuts, the way a holy woman covers her arms in animal blood. She's cursing curses to waken the dead.

WOCKY. So she's back to see Pompey's Triumph.

FLOOD. Is that what she's come back for?

WOCKY. She hasn't come back for me.

Beat.

FLOOD. Will you come?

WOCKY. Come and what – watch? *Yes I'll come* – come on then, let me see the worst.

WOCKY *goes. Then* FLOOD.

Scene Four

MACU *comes on, cut to ribbons, with a crowd round her. They're throwing salt and lentils at her, and generally tormenting her. For her part, MACU is using them to whip herself into a frenzy, goading them so they'll goad her more.*

MACU. I've seen things, I've seen visions, I've seen you in my visions. The boy prince took me to the mountaintop and told me to look. And I saw you. And you were eating stones. And you were so hungry you thought you were eating loaves. And the boy prince laughed his head off and said, tell them the bad news. – I see visions with my teeth.

MAN. Visions!

WOMAN. Visions!? I *know* her! She was one of the wailers. She used to live over there before the fire gutted it.

MACU. Fire? Where?

WOMAN. Show the woman where the fire was.

A child goes to point out where the fire was.

CHILD. There.

MACU. There?

CHILD. First it was all burned down, then the men came along and flattened it.

MACU. Is this the place?

MAN. What did you expect, a cemetery?

WOMAN. Now they're building that.

MAN 2. Ten storeys high that will be.

MAN. That's until it falls down.

MACU. Oh Laura. – Come on, the dead. Come on, the dead. Pompey's back.

WOMAN. What's she saying now?

CHILD. She's talking to the dead.

They start throwing salt and lentils at her again.

MACU. Come on, the dead. Listen to that, the hissing of salt, the rattle of lentils, that's the rattle of the dead having a natter. Wait till Pompey hears that and a voice whispers in his ear, here come the dead. His prick will shrink away inside him, it won't even come out to piss. He'll hear the blood in his brains and he'll shrink away like a man's prick in the cold.

FLOOD and WOCKY come on. They stand at a distance and watch.

MACU. Come on, the dead. Pompey's back. Pompey's back and these clowns have taken a holiday.

CHILD. They gave us a holiday.

MAN 2. What do you want us to do, work it?

MACU. Cry! Wail!

They 'cry', 'wail'. MACU starts to cover herself in a grey dust, street dust.

FLOOD. Are you going to stand there and watch her?

WOCKY. She's in ribbons.

MACU. So come on, the dead. Come on, the dead: Pompey's back. Let's go and rattle his door.

WOMAN. And what are you going to do – spit in his face?

MACU. Tsssssst!

WOMAN. Spit in his face?

MACU. Tssssssst! Like a snake! There's so much poison in me, my spit is poisonous!

MAN. On you go then.

MAN 2. Yes. On you go.

MAN. Speak to him. He's another sad bastard, you and him would get on.

MACU. I don't even want to speak the same language as him. If I say a word, if I say *grief* he'll think, *grief*, I know what that means. Then it would be like we shared a tongue! I'd rather take my tongue out and stamp it into the dirt.

MACU *applies some more dust to her bloodied skin.*

FLOOD. Speak to her.

WOCKY. Speak? All she'd see is my mouth open and shut, a hole in my face.

MACU. The dead are coming, Pompey. The dead are coming.

WOMAN. On you go then. Kill him.

MAN. Yes. Kill him.

WOMAN. Imagine she did.

MAN. Kill him.

WOMAN. Please. For us.

MAN 2. Who's got a knife? Don't worry about his bodyguards, they'll take one look at you and run.

WOMAN. They'll come screaming past us with their brains running out their ears.

MAN 2. Who's got a knife?

WOCKY. I have.

He walks across to MACU *and gives her the knife.*

Kill him, Macu. Kill him.

MACU *looks at him.*

WOMAN. Come on, the dead.

MAN. Come on, the dead.

MACU. Come on, the dead. Sit up, rattle your bones, come for a walk.

And she exits, followed by her tormentors, still throwing rubbish at her.

FLOOD. He'll kill her.

WOCKY. Will he? She'll walk through them, crowds, bodyguards, she'll walk right through them. I *know* her, remember. She's Macu: she can walk through swords!

He exits in same direction as MACU. FLOOD *follows.*

Scene Five

POMPEY, *followed by* CRASSUS, MARCELLA *and* SORCHA.

POMPEY. I'm sorry, Crassus. I can't do it.

SORCHA. Pompey, the crowd's waiting for you.

CRASSUS. They're getting restless.

POMPEY. Clear the streets then. Tell the senate I won't enter Rome till the streets are deserted.

MARCELLA. Oh, yawn!

POMPEY. Oh Marcella, just leave me. Don't torment yourself. – When this city was great, women made swords. Now they're the same as everyone else. They're spectators. Tax-shirkers!

MARCELLA. Tax-shirkers!

POMPEY. Because who pays? You? You? No, you spectate!

MARCELLA. 'Tax-shirkers'? You've lost me.

POMPEY. I've told you: I'm sick. Not sick, nauseous. The whole point is I'm *not* sick. If I was sick that would explain it. I'm fine! Perfect! I just want to put my hand down my throat and pull my stomach out. And you want me to walk through that mob?

Young OFFICER *enters.*

OFFICER. Pompey. They've arrested a woman in the crowd and taken a dagger off her. She was cursing you like a holy woman. The crowd were frightened of her, they touched their lucky charms and let her past.

POMPEY. And where is she now? Bring her here, I want to see her.

OFFICER *exits*.

SORCHA. Pompey. People are fainting out there. The crowd see them being carried away on stretchers and think they're dead. So then they start a punch-up.

CRASSUS. Drunk men in the sun, who knows what way they'll turn. – The crowd is vast, Pompey!

POMPEY. Ho. Popular? I was the kind of boy who used to ingratiate himself with the other boys. What about you, Crassus?

CRASSUS. No.

POMPEY. You remember the type though? Boys who tried too hard. There was a boy at school: Lucius. I wanted to be friends with him. Then one summer he invited me to stay with him. He was the most popular boy in the world. So – summer! – fishing – swimming in the river – boys! And then one day we were wrestling, and when they dragged me off him he was dead. – Well, he wasn't dead but I *thought* he was dead. Everyone did. I'd throttled him. – You can only try so hard before it becomes humiliating.

OFFICER *enters with* MACU.

OFFICER. This is the woman here, Pompey.

POMPEY *turns to look*.

MARCELLA. Oh.

POMPEY. Look at her.

CRASSUS. Raw.

MARCELLA. She can't put her arms down by her side.

OFFICER. You can see her meat.

POMPEY. And does she speak?

OFFICER. Yes. She speaks.

POMPEY. She speaks? Because she looks how *I* feel! Grief.

MARCELLA. Remember she had a dagger, Pompey.

POMPEY. Only with me there's nothing to show it. There's not a single mark on me.

MARCELLA. Don't go too close.

POMPEY. So you speak? Do you prophesy? Don't tell me I'll come to a bad end, I know that. So what do you do, curses? Omens? – Oh this is boring, let's go, I can hear the crowd shouting for me.

MACU. You burnt my throat.

POMPEY. She spoke.

MACU. You burnt my throat.

POMPEY. Shhhh! She's speaking.

MACU. I was a wailer. We refused to mourn for Sulla. Then there was a fire.

POMPEY. Was there?

MACU. My daughter died. Laura.

POMPEY. And what's your name?

MACU. Macu.

SORCHA. She was one of the wailers that came to your house that night.

POMPEY. We're quits then. Grief.

MACU. Grief. What do you know?

POMPEY. I was at my father's funeral. I saw the mob tear him into six pieces. I was ten at the time, I could count. – Here.

He gives her a dagger.

Take it.

MARCELLA. Pompey!

POMPEY. It's a ceremonial dagger, of course. But it works. Try it.

MARCELLA. Does everything have to happen twice?

POMPEY. Twice?

MARCELLA. Don't turn your back on her!

POMPEY. Twice? Everything has to happen again and again and again.

OFFICER. I'll go get help.

POMPEY. There's no end to it.

He says that line with his back to MACU. *Then he turns to her.*

So here we are. She's defenceless. So is he. So am I, for that matter.

He turns away again.

Danger! It's worth it just to see the look on your faces. You're not spectators now. You can't bribe your way out of this.

CRASSUS. The crowd, Pompey –

MARCELLA. Will someone take that knife off her!

POMPEY. Shhhh!

CRASSUS. They're booing.

POMPEY. They're booing.

MACU. Applause, Pompey, isn't it deafening? Will I tell you a dream I had?

POMPEY. Is it an omen?

MACU. We all went to a feast, there were thirty five plates and on every plate was a human tongue. Then all the tongues got up on their hind legs and clapped you.

POMPEY. Listen. They're cheering again.

MARCELLA. I hope they tear you apart!

POMPEY. Ho!

MARCELLA. *What are you doing to us?*

MACU. They have torn him apart, they've torn him into a hundred thousand pieces. Applause, Pompey – a lover could be whispering in your ear and you wouldn't hear what she said, you'd be listening to the silence outside and worrying. You hear applause and your eyes scatter. Your brains scatter.

POMPEY. Oh, listen, can I have my dagger back? You're not going to use it. Unless you're going to use it.

MACU. Applause, Pompey – are you listening? Are you listening? This is the loudest applause you'll hear, ever –

She cuts her throat.

The blood jets out. Screams etc. POMPEY *turns away from her with blood all over him, his face.*

MACU. Pompey! Pompey!

POMPEY. Get her out of here!

MARCELLA. Don't go near her.

POMPEY. Blood. Warm blood.

OFFICER *enters, armed.*

MARCELLA. She's still alive!

MACU *dies.*

CRASSUS. She's dead.

Pause.

MARCELLA. Horrible. Horrible.

CRASSUS. It's over.

MARCELLA. I could hear the blood gargling in her throat.

POMPEY. She gargled my name.

MARCELLA. She stood there blurting blood from her mouth like a fountain.

Pause.

SORCHA. Pompey. The crowd want you. – We'll tell the people a sacrifice was offered. And a priest washed you in sacrificial blood.

POMPEY. I'm polluted.

SORCHA. Anointed.

POMPEY. Her last words were my name.

CRASSUS. We have to go, Pompey. We can think about it later.

POMPEY. 'Pompey'. I hear that name and I think, who's that? I don't know who you're all talking about half the time. – Come on then. Let's go.

They exit.

Scene Six

FLOOD *and* WOCKY *and* EMILIA *come on with a funeral stretcher.*

FLOOD. They say her last words were his name.

WOCKY. Pompey.

FLOOD. Pompey.

WOCKY. Let's get her lifted and away from here, hurry.

EMILIA. Take your time. We'll go to my house first, keep her to ourselves for a little while. Then we'll walk her to the cemetery. We'll cry till the chains drop from round our throats.

They arrange her on the stretcher and cover her in a white sheet. Then they stand back, as if they're around a grave. They're very still. They don't look at each other when they speak, directing everything through MACU.

WOCKY. I gave her the knife. It was me that gave her the knife.

EMILIA. Don't, Wocky, or it'll never end. – Speak to her. Tell her something.

FLOOD. Things tell me that I'm old now, Macu, since I lost my husband in the fire. But I still try and live, day to day. – When bad things happen to you, the only way to get better is to do good things. People can be kind to you, people can listen to you, people can love you. But it's not enough. The only way to get better is to do good things. – I'm saying this to you too, Wocky. So you can live your life.

WOCKY. You were lovely, Macu. I used to smile just to look at you. Remember the night we walked into the woods together? We took off our skins that night. I went there the next day, I never told you this, I went there the next day. I think I thought I'd find two skins lying under a tree. – Speak to Laura. Tell her you love her. Tell her I love her.

Beat.

EMILIA. Let's take her away now.

Nobody moves.

further ahead than just ('money'!) than just today. You write
your story and (Danny Glasgow today said): correct? I'm half
way there.

LUCY. Well if you're sure . . . fine.

And that's SAMMY: *fucked.*

SAMMY. Fine.

LUCY. I mean: brilliant. Thank you.

SAMMY. Brilliant. Great. You want some flesh, I'm your man. –
If you'll just step over to the taxi then (great).

LUCY. Thank you.

She goes.

SAMMY (*as she goes*). First stop: Parkhead Forge. – See? Did you
see that? I hope that opened your eyes, ya wee pagans. Things
happen for me.

And off he goes.
SUSAN *slowly goes to the edge of the stage. She will watch* SAMMY
and LUCY *walk all the way to the taxi, totally absorbed.*

TRACKY. You don't see him, Susan.

SUSAN. He's so passionate.

TRACKY. I look at him close.

SUSAN. He's so tempestuous.

TRACKY. I look at him in detail.

TRACKY *speaks to* SUSAN's *unlistening back.*

You should see him when he cries. That's the worst. I can't
look. Because see human flesh, see when it's burned, see when
it's grilled and the skin's like healing up and then it starts to
cry, it starts to leak like these really disgusting tears? That's
how *obsequious* he is. – Same last night. I'm lying in my bed
listening. I can hear him. Her. Then it goes quiet.

Quiet.

Then it goes quiet. That's the worst. It goes quiet and my
stomach turns to mud, because I know. Then the door opens
and – shouting – and she's pushing the door in his face but
then she runs down the corridor and *that's* when my stomach

turns to mud – not when I said – *then* – and she's in the bathroom and locked the door. And he's after her, he's outside the door like *begging* her and saying he's sorry, and I just switch off.

A taxi door slams, then another.

I just switch off. And then he's got his face up against the bathroom window – Agnes, Agnes – and she smashes right into it with a hammer.

Taxi goes.

Then it's morning. You wake up clear as a bell and you think what happened?

SUSAN *turns to look at* TRACKY.

SUSAN. They've gone.

TRACKY (*switched off*). Then you go to the bathroom. Only it's different from what you expect. There's just these broken bits of glass. And you can see right through the window, like you can see the toilet clear as a bell through the broken window. It only lasts about three seconds. And then it's like, so what?

SUSAN. I know. What'll we do now?

TRACKY *shrugs.*

TRACKY. I wish something exciting would happen.

SUSAN. I know. Will we follow them? We could get the train to Parkhead.

TRACKY *shrugs.*

TRACKY. Right.

SUSAN. Because we might as well.

TRACKY. Right. Come on then.

They go.

TEX *comes on. Stands there, amused, as the scene changes round about him. Then he exits.*